CALCULUS
AND
PROBABILITY

FOR ACTUARIAL STUDENTS

I0434861

BY

ALFRED HENRY, F.I.A.

PUBLISHED BY THE AUTHORITY AND ON BEHALF OF

THE INSTITUTE OF ACTUARIES

BY

CHARLES & EDWIN LAYTON, FARRINGDON STREET, E.C. 4

LONDON

ISBN: 978-0-359-08567-5

INTRODUCTION

ACTUARIAL science is peculiarly dependent upon the Theory of Probabilities, the solution of many of its problems is best effected by resort to the Differential and Integral Calculus and in practical work the Calculus of Finite Differences is almost indispensable. Excellent text-books on these subjects are, of course, available but none of them has been written with the special requirements of the actuary in view. In beginning his training the student is, therefore, confronted by the difficulty of judicious selection and in the circumstances it has appeared to the Council of the Institute of Actuaries that a mathematical text-book sufficiently comprehensive, with the standard works on Higher Algebra, to provide the ground-work of an actuarial education would be of great value. At the request of the Council, Mr Alfred Henry has undertaken the preparation of such a work and the resulting volume is issued in the confident expectation that it will materially lighten the toil of those who essay to qualify themselves for an actuarial career.

A. W. W.

May 1922.

AUTHOR'S PREFACE

ACTUARIAL science is essentially practical in that, whilst it is based on the processes of pure mathematics, the object of the worker must be to produce a numerical result.

For this reason it is necessary for considerable prominence to be given, in the curriculum of the actuarial student, to the subject of Finite Differences, and it thus becomes convenient, in the study of those subjects not included under the heading of Algebra, to deal with this part of the syllabus first and, notwithstanding certain theoretical objections, to treat the fundamental propositions of the Differential and the Integral Calculus as being, substantially, special cases of similar propositions in Finite Differences. The subjects enumerated cover so wide a field that it has been necessary to exercise considerable compression and to include only such problems as are requisite for a proper knowledge of the subjects within the syllabus.

In the chapter on Probability it will be seen that the numerical or "frequency" theory of probability has been adopted. Having regard to the practical nature of the actuary's work, it is thought that strict adherence to this aspect of the subject is necessary if the student is to acquire sound views from the outset. The subject of Inverse Probability has been excluded from the examination syllabus in recent years and for this reason it is not introduced into the present work.

In conclusion the author would wish to tender his best thanks to many colleagues and other members of the Institute of Actuaries for their kind assistance and useful criticisms. In this connection he is particularly indebted to Mr G. J. Lidstone, who was good enough to read the chapters relating to Finite Differences and made many valuable suggestions.

A. H.

August 1922.

CONTENTS

CHAPTER I

FUNCTIONS. DEFINITION OF CERTAIN TERMS. GRAPHICAL REPRESENTATION

1. When the value of a certain quantity y depends upon, or bears a fixed relation to that of another quantity, x, y is said to be a *function of* x, and the relationship is written as $y = f(x)$.

[Other notations used are u_x, v_x, $\phi(x)$, etc.]

Thus, we may have $y = x^3$, $y = a^x$, $y = \sin x$, $y = \log x$. The quantities forming the right-hand sides of the equations are all functions of x.

When expressed in this way the relationship of y to x is said to be *explicit*. But if, for example, $ax^2 + 2bxy + cy^2 = 0$, it is clear that, whilst the value of y depends upon that of x, it cannot be determined in any case by direct substitution of the value of x. The relationship in such circumstances is said to be *implicit*. In this particular example the relationship can, of course, be made *explicit* by solving the equation for y in terms of x.

The quantities x and y are called *variables*.

The quantity x is called the *independent variable* since it may assume any value, whereas y is called the *dependent variable* since its value depends upon that of x.

The independent variable is sometimes referred to as the *argument*.

2. Functions may, of course, involve more than one variable. For example we may have $y = x^2 z^3$ or $u = \dfrac{x^2 \log y}{z}$; and all these variables may be involved implicitly. A function of more than one variable would be denoted by $f(x, y, z)$, $u_{x:y}$, etc.

If we have a function u, such that

$$u = x^a y^b z^c + x^{a'} y^{b'} z^{c'} + \dots$$

and

$$a + b + c = a' + b' + c' = \dots = n,$$

then u is said to be a *homogeneous function of n dimensions*.

Rectilinear Co-ordinates.

3. A function of two variables may be represented graphically according to the scheme of the figure shown.

Let two straight lines of indefinite length OX, OY be drawn at right angles to each other. The point O is called the *origin*, OX is called the *axis of x* and OY the *axis of y*.

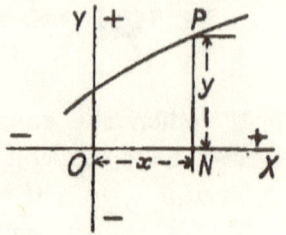

Then if ON is measured along the axis of x, equal in value to x, and at that point a perpendicular line PN is drawn equal in value to $y = f(x)$, ON is called the *abscissa* and PN the *ordinate* of the point P. The convention is taken that measurements of x in the direction OX are considered to be positive and those in the contrary direction negative. Similarly measurements of y in the direction OY are treated as positive and those in the contrary direction as negative. The point P, written for convenience as (x, y), is thus completely determined from given values of x and y.

If for every value of x the corresponding value of y were plotted on a diagram such as the above a continuous curve would be obtained which would be the graphical representation of the equation $y = f(x)$. It is, of course, impossible in practice to plot every value of the function, but generally a few values can be filled in so as to enable the curve to be drawn by sight.

It should be noted that the lines OX and OY, and consequently the origin O, can be chosen quite arbitrarily and that the position of the point P can be fixed, in the manner indicated, with reference to any suitable axes of co-ordinates.

4. The point P can be fixed with reference to its distance from two straight lines not at right angles to each other, the distance $PN = y$ being measured along a line parallel to the axis of y.

The values x and y corresponding to a given point P are called the *rectilinear co-ordinates* (or simply the *co-ordinates*) of the point P. Where the axes are at right angles to each other the system can be distinguished, if necessary, by referring to x and y as the *rectangular co-ordinates of P*.

As a rule rectangular co-ordinates are the more convenient to use in practice and lead to simpler results. Unless otherwise expressed it is to be understood that rectangular co-ordinates are implied.

5. The following examples give simple cases of the graphical representation of explicit functions.

(i) The equation $x = a$ clearly represents a straight line parallel to the axis of y and at distance a from it; for the value of x at any point is constant and equal to a.

(ii) The equation $y = mx$ represents a straight line passing through the origin and making an angle θ with the axis of x, where $\tan \theta = m$; since at any point the ratio $y : x$ is constant and equal to $\tan \theta$.

(iii)

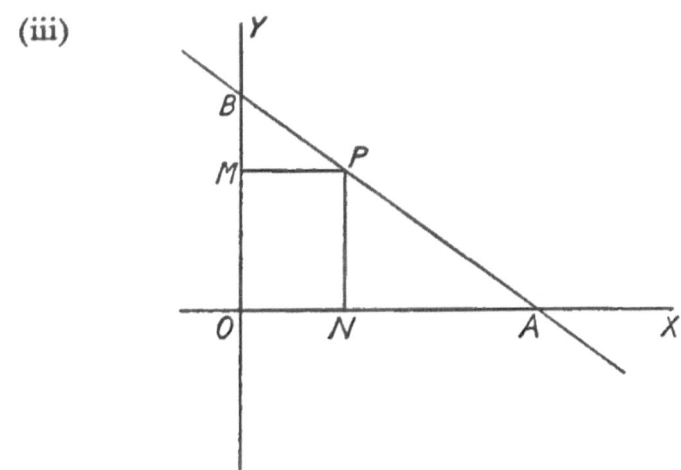

Let AB be any straight line cutting the axes of x and y respectively at the points A and B, so that $OA = a$ and $OB = b$.

Let P be any point on the line AB, of which the co-ordinates are (x, y). Then, if perpendiculars PN and PM be dropped upon the axes of x and y, $MP = x$ and $NP = y$.

Also
$$\frac{x}{a} = \frac{ON}{OA} = \frac{PB}{AB}$$

and
$$\frac{y}{b} = \frac{NP}{OB} = \frac{AP}{AB},$$

∴
$$\frac{x}{a} + \frac{y}{b} = \frac{PB + AP}{AB}$$
$$= 1.$$

Hence $\dfrac{x}{a} + \dfrac{y}{b} = 1$ is the equation of the straight line AB.

6. An implicit function can be similarly represented. For example, it is obvious from the ordinary properties of the circle that the implicit relationship $x^2 + y^2 = a^2$ represents a circle of radius a with its centre at the origin.

Note. The function $y = a + bx + cx^2 + dx^3 + \ldots$ is sometimes called a *parabolic* function, since the equation $y = a + bx + cx^2$ is represented graphically by a curve which is known as a parabola.

7. It does not follow that for every value of x there will always be a real value of y.

Thus, consider the function $y^2 = (x - a)(x - b)(x - c)$, where $c > b > a$. If x is negative, the right-hand side of the equation is negative and y can have no real value. If x is positive and $< a$, the position is the same. If, however, $x > a$ and $< b$, then the right-hand side is positive and y has a real value; but when $x > b$ and $< c$, y is again unreal and remains so until $x > c$ when a real value of y results for each value of x.

The form of the curve is shown below, where $OA = a$, $OB = b$ and $OC = c$.

In circumstances such as these, where one or more parts of a curve are isolated from the others, the function and the curve representing it are said to be *discontinuous*.

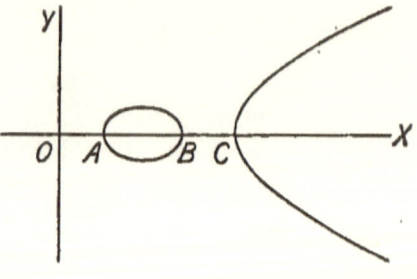

8. It is convenient here to introduce the conception of the *limiting value* of a function, or simply a *limit*.

If $y = f(x)$ and y continuously tends towards a certain value and can be made to differ by as little as we please from that value, by assigning a suitable value to x, say a, then $f(a)$ is said to be the limiting value of $f(x)$ when x tends to the value a.

A convenient notation is as follows:

$$y \rightarrow f(a) \text{ when } x \rightarrow a.$$

Also $f(a)$ would be expressed as $\underset{x \rightarrow a}{\text{Lt}} f(x).$

Thus let $y = \dfrac{x-a}{x}$. By writing y in the form $1 - \dfrac{a}{x}$ we see that by making x indefinitely great, we can make the value of y differ from unity by as little as we please.

Thus
$$\underset{x \to \infty}{\text{Lt}} \ \frac{x-a}{x} = 1.$$

9. We will now give an example of another form of discontinuity, and for this purpose we will take the curve $y = \left(\dfrac{x}{x-a}\right)^2$ shown below.

Here it will be seen that as $x \to a$, the value of $y \to \infty$. Similarly if $x \to \infty$, $y \to 1$.

Thus if we draw two lines, one PN parallel to the axis of y and at distance a from it, and the other QM parallel to the axis of x and at unit distance from it, the curve will continuously approach these lines but will not actually touch them except at an infinite distance from the origin.

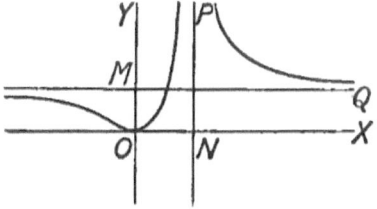

Such lines are called *asymptotes* to the curve.

In general, actuarial functions are finite and continuous; but in mathematical work, as will be seen later, attention to these points is necessary in the consideration of certain problems.

10. Explicit functions involving two variables, and implicit functions of three variables, can be expressed in a diagram of three dimensions. Thus if we have $z = f(x, y)$ or $f(x, y, z) = 0$ we may measure x, y and z by reference to their perpendicular distance, not from two lines, but from three planes at right angles to each other.

A useful simile is that of the floor and two adjacent walls of a rectangular room of indefinite size. Any point in space is fixed by reference to its perpendicular distance from the two walls and the floor, x and y being the respective distances from the walls, and z that from the floor. The conventions as to positive and negative values are similar to those previously explained.

11. As an example, if $z = x^2 y^2$, the values of the function for unit intervals in the values of x and y are shown in the following table:

Value of y	Value of x					
	0	1	2	3	4	...
0	0	0	0	0	0	...
1	0	1	4	9	16	...
2	0	4	16	36	64	...
3	0	9	36	81	144	...
4	0	16	64	144	256	...
⋮	⋮	⋮	⋮	⋮	⋮	

We will conceive the floor as being covered with a linoleum of chess-board pattern, the sides of the squares being at unit distance apart. The perpendicular distance from the floor of all points in these squares is nil and, therefore, z has the value 0. The corners of these squares will thus represent the various points $(0, 0, 0)$, $(0, 1, 0)$, $(1, 1, 0)$, $(1, 0, 0)$, $(2, 1, 0)$, etc. If we were to erect at each corner a peg of height equal to the appropriate figure taken from the above table, the tops of the pegs would give points on the surface representing the equation $z = x^2 y^2$. If the value of z were plotted for every possible combination of values of x and y, we should, of course, obtain the continuous surface corresponding to $z = x^2 y^2$.

Polar Co-ordinates.

12. An alternative method of defining a point in a plane surface is as follows.

Let an origin O be taken and a fixed line OX be drawn from it; then the position of any point P is known if the distance OP and the angle XOP are given.

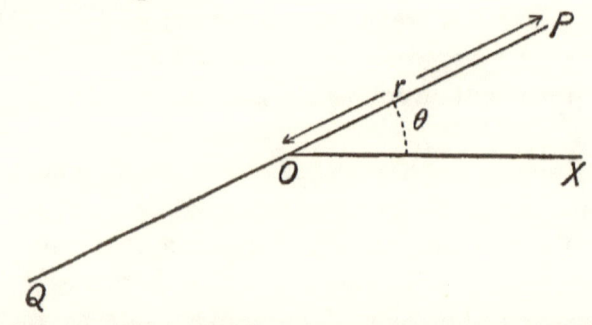

Thus if $OP = r$ and $\angle XOP = \theta$, r and θ are known as the *polar*

co-ordinates of P, and the point P can be written as (r, θ). The distance OP is called the *radius vector* and the angle XOP is called the *vectorial angle*.

The convention adopted is that the angle XOP is reckoned positive if measured from OX in a direction contrary to that in which the hands of a clock revolve, and negative if measured in the reverse direction.

Further, the radius vector is considered positive if measured from O along a line bounding the vectorial angle, and negative if measured in the opposite direction. To illustrate this system, let PO be produced to a point Q such that $OQ = OP = r$. Then the point Q may be written alternatively as $(r, \pi + \theta)$ or $(-r, \theta)$.

13. The relation between rectangular and polar co-ordinates can be easily established. For if OX be taken as the axis of x then OY, the axis of y, is perpendicular to it. Also let PN be drawn from the point P perpendicular to the axis of x.

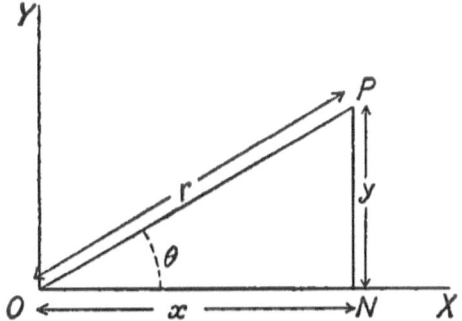

Then, clearly, if x, y be the rectangular co-ordinates of P,

$$x = ON = OP \cos \theta = r \cos \theta,$$
$$y = PN = OP \sin \theta = r \sin \theta.$$

Any equation in rectangular co-ordinates can therefore be transformed into an equation in polar co-ordinates by the above substitutions.

14. Three simple examples of the graphical representation of an equation in polar co-ordinates are now given.

(i) The polar equation $r = a$ clearly represents a circle of radius a with its centre at the origin; since the radius vector is constant and equal to a.

(ii) In the diagram shown in § 13, if $ON = a$ and PN be produced indefinitely in either direction, then the polar equation of the straight line so obtained will be

$$r \cos \theta = a,$$

since if P be any point in the line

$$OP \cos \theta = r \cos \theta = ON = a.$$

(iii) Let OA be a diameter of a circle OPA of radius a. Then if P be any point on the circle such that $OP = r$ and $\angle AOP = \theta$, $OP = OA \cos \theta = 2a \cos \theta$.

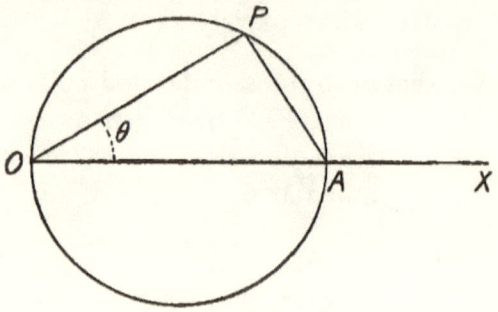

The polar equation of the circle, if O be the origin, is therefore

$$r = 2a \cos \theta.$$

CHAPTER II

FINITE DIFFERENCES. DEFINITIONS

1. The subject or calculus of Finite Differences deals with the changes in the values of a function (the dependent variable) arising from finite changes in the value of the independent variable (see Chapter I, § 1).

Many questions arise which can be dealt with on systematic lines, but probably the most important problems which require to be solved in actual practice, and with which we are concerned at this stage of the subject, are the summation of series, and the insertion of missing terms in a series of which only certain terms are given.

It will be convenient to proceed in the first place to some elementary conceptions and definitions.

2. If we have a series consisting of a number of values of a function, corresponding to equidistant values of the independent variable, and from each term of the series we subtract the algebraic value of the immediately preceding term, we shall obtain a further series of equidistant terms. The process is known as *differencing* the terms of the series, and the terms of the new series are known as the *first differences* of the original terms. By repeating the process with the terms forming the first differences, we shall obtain a further series forming the *second differences* of the original function, and so on. Thus if we have $f(x)$ for the first term of the series and $f(x+h)$ for the second term, the first difference of $f(x)$ is $f(x+h) - f(x)$ and is designated $\Delta f(x)$. The second difference of $f(x)$ is $\Delta f(x+h) - \Delta f(x)$ and is designated $\Delta^2 f(x)$. This may be set out as in the following scheme:

Function	First Differences	Second Differences	Third Differences
$f(x)$	$f(x+h) - f(x)$	$f(x+2h) - 2f(x+h) + f(x)$	$f(x+3h) - 3f(x+2h) + 3f(x+h) - f(x)$
$f(x+h)$	$f(x+2h) - f(x+h)$	$f(x+3h) - 2f(x+2h) + f(x+h)$	$f(x+4h) - 3f(x+3h) + 3f(x+2h) - f(x+h)$
$f(x+2h)$	$f(x+3h) - f(x+2h)$	$f(x+4h) - 2f(x+3h) + f(x+2h)$	$\vdots$
$f(x+3h)$	$f(x+4h) - f(x+3h)$	$\vdots$	
$f(x+4h)$	$\vdots$		
$\vdots$			

The first term of the series is known as the *leading term* and the terms in the top line of differences are known as the *leading differences* of the series.

It must be clearly understood at the outset that Δ is *merely a symbol* representing the operation of differencing $f(x)$ once; it is in no sense a coefficient by which $f(x)$ is multiplied. This point is dealt with again in § 5.

3. An examination of the character of the series which ultimately results from the process of differencing repeatedly, leads to the development of certain important theorems. Before proceeding further, it will be helpful to give a practical example.

Example 1. Obtain the differences of the series given by $f(x) = x^3$, where x has all integral values from 1 to 6.

x	$f(x)$	First Differences	Second Differences	Third Differences	Fourth Differences
1	1	7	12	6	0
2	8	19	18	6	0
3	27	37	24	6	
4	64	61	30		
5	125	91			
6	216				

It will be observed in the above example that the fourth and, therefore, all higher differences are zero; it will be seen later that this would equally have been the case had more terms of the series been taken. We can therefore construct all the remaining terms of the series by a process of continuous addition.

4. Although most functions with which the actuary has to deal are not of the simple character of that shown above, yet it will usually be found that the differences of the function for which further values are required tend to the value zero and are susceptible to treatment by methods which will be developed subsequently.

The student should obtain confirmation of this fact and insight into the character of certain series by taking out the differences of tabulated functions such as logarithms, annuity-values, etc.

5. Before proceeding to the consideration of the various problems which arise, it is necessary to develop certain fundamental formulas.

In § 2 Δ has already been defined as the symbol of the operation by means of which the value of $f(x+h)-f(x)$ is obtained. Similarly, it is customary to use the symbol E as representing the operation by which the value of $f(x)$ is changed to the value $f(x+h)$, so that

$$Ef(x) = f(x+h) = f(x) + \Delta f(x).$$

It must be carefully remembered that these symbols represent *operations* only and must be interpreted accordingly. Thus $E^2 x^2$ is clearly not the equivalent of $(Ex)^2$; the former expresses the result of operating twice upon the function x^2 in the manner indicated above, giving a value $(x+2h)^2$, whereas in the latter case the operation is applied once to the function x and the resulting term $(x+h)$ is squared.

6. If, then, these symbols are found to obey the ordinary algebraical laws, they can be dealt with algebraically provided always that the results are interpreted symbolically in relation to the function which is the subject of the operation. This principle is known as that of Separation of Symbols or Calculus of Operations.

The algebraic laws referred to above comprise:

(1) The Law of Distribution.

(2) The Law of Indices.

(3) The Law of Commutation.

Taking these laws in succession:

(1) The symbol Δ is *distributive* in its operation, for

$$\Delta[f_1(x)+f_2(x)+f_3(x)+\ldots] = [f_1(x+h)+f_2(x+h)+f_3(x+h)+\ldots]$$
$$-[f_1(x)+f_2(x)+f_3(x)+\ldots]$$
$$= [f_1(x+h)-f_1(x)]+[f_2(x+h)-f_2(x)]$$
$$+[f_3(x+h)-f_3(x)]+\ldots$$
$$= \Delta f_1(x)+\Delta f_2(x)+\Delta f_3(x)+\ldots.$$

Similarly the symbol E is *distributive*, for

$$E[f_1(x)+f_2(x)+f_3(x)+\ldots] = [f_1(x+h)+f_2(x+h)+f_3(x+h)+\ldots]$$
$$= Ef_1(x)+Ef_2(x)+Ef_3(x)+\ldots.$$

(2) The symbol Δ obeys the *law of indices*, for in the case of positive integers the symbol $\Delta^m f(x)$ represents the operation, repeated m times, of differencing $f(x)$.

Thus $\Delta^m f(x) = (\Delta\Delta\Delta \ldots m \text{ times}) f(x),$

$\therefore \;\; \Delta^n \Delta^m f(x) = (\Delta\Delta\Delta \ldots n \text{ times})(\Delta\Delta\Delta \ldots m \text{ times}) f(x)$

$$= (\Delta\Delta\Delta \ldots (m+n) \text{ times}) f(x)$$

$$= \Delta^{n+m} f(x).$$

Similarly it may be shown that the symbol E obeys the *law of indices*.

(3) The symbol Δ is *commutative* in its operation as regards constants, for, if c be a constant,

$$\Delta[cf(x)] = cf(x+h) - cf(x)$$

$$= c[f(x+h) - f(x)]$$

$$= c\,\Delta f(x).$$

The like result can be deduced as regards E.

7. It follows that, since

$$Ef(x) = (1 + \Delta)f(x),$$

therefore $E = 1 + \Delta$

and $\Delta = E - 1.$

The two operators are thus connected by a simple relation, which will be found later to lead to important results.

8. As an example of the manner in which the relationship between the operations represented by E and Δ can be utilised in the solution of problems, we may take the following:

Example 2. Prove that

$$f(0) + xf(1) + \frac{x^2}{2!}f(2) + \frac{x^3}{3!}f(3) + \ldots$$

$$= e^x\left[f(0) + x\Delta f(0) + \frac{x^2}{2!}\Delta^2 f(0) + \ldots\right].$$

Since

$$f(1) = Ef(0) = (1+\Delta)f(0);\; f(2) = E^2 f(0) = (1+\Delta)^2 f(0), \text{ etc.,}$$

we have $f(0) + xf(1) + \dfrac{x^2}{2!}f(2) + \dfrac{x^3}{3!}f(3) + \ldots$

$$= \left[1 + x(1+\Delta) + \frac{x^2}{2!}(1+\Delta)^2 + \ldots\right]f(0)$$

$$= \left[e^{x(1+\Delta)}\right]f(0)$$

$$= e^x\left[e^{x\Delta}\right]f(0)$$

$$= e^x\left[1 + x\Delta + x^2\frac{\Delta^2}{2!} + \ldots\right]f(0)$$

$$= e^x\left[f(0) + x\Delta f(0) + \frac{x^2}{2!}\Delta^2 f(0) + \ldots\right].$$

CHAPTER III

FINITE DIFFERENCES. GENERAL FORMULAS
AND SPECIAL CASES

1. Starting from the relationship proved in Chapter II, § 7, it is now possible to develop two formulas of the utmost importance.

2. *To express $f(x + mh)$ in terms of $f(x)$ and its leading differences.*

By definition
$$f(x + mh) = E^m f(x)$$
$$= (1 + \Delta)^m f(x),$$
since by Chapter II, § 7, $\qquad E = 1 + \Delta.$

Expanding the above expression by the Binomial Theorem we have

$$f(x + mh) = \left[1 + m\Delta + \binom{m}{2}\Delta^2 + \binom{m}{3}\Delta^3 + \dots + \binom{m}{m}\Delta^m\right]f(x)$$

$$= f(x) + m\Delta f(x) + \binom{m}{2}\Delta^2 f(x) + \binom{m}{3}\Delta^3 f(x) + \dots$$

$$+ \binom{m}{m}\Delta^m f(x) \dots\dots(1).$$

Bearing in mind that the symbol Δ obeys the ordinary algebraic laws and that the Binomial Theorem holds for all values of the index, positive, fractional or negative, it will be realised that the above proof is perfectly general.

It is instructive, however, to show how the formula may be deduced for fractional and for negative values of m.

3. *Fractional value.* Let $\dfrac{m}{n}$ be a positive proper fraction, and let the interval between the given terms of the series be h. It is required to find the value of $f\left(x + \dfrac{m}{n}h\right)$.

Also let $\qquad f(x + h) - f(x) = \Delta f(x),$

and $\qquad f\left(x + \dfrac{h}{n}\right) - f(x) = \delta f(x).$

In the second case, the unit of differencing has been altered to $\frac{h}{n}$ and, bearing in mind that n is a positive integer, we may write at once from the theorem in the preceding article

$$f(x+h) = (1+\delta)^n f(x),$$

therefore

$$(1+\Delta)f(x) = (1+\delta)^n f(x),$$

and

$$(1+\Delta)^{\frac{1}{n}} f(x) = (1+\delta)f(x).$$

Since m is also an integer, it follows that

$$(1+\delta)^m f(x) = f\left(x + \frac{m}{n} h\right) = (1+\Delta)^{\frac{m}{n}} f(x)$$

$$= \left[1 + \frac{m}{n}\Delta + \binom{\frac{m}{n}}{2}\Delta^2 + \ldots\right] f(x)$$

$$= f(x) + \frac{m}{n}\Delta f(x) + \binom{\frac{m}{n}}{2}\Delta^2 f(x) + \ldots.$$

4. *Negative value.* It is desired to find the value of $f(x-mh)$. Now, from the preceding theorems, it is clear that

$$(1+\Delta)^m f(x-mh) = f(x),$$

therefore

$$f(x-mh) = (1+\Delta)^{-m} f(x)$$

$$= \left[1 + (-m)\Delta + \binom{-m}{2}\Delta^2 + \ldots\right] f(x)$$

$$= f(x) + (-m)\Delta f(x) + \binom{-m}{2}\Delta^2 f(x) + \ldots.$$

The above proofs show that the theorem holds universally and illustrate how the principle of Separation of Symbols can be applied whenever the symbols of operation obey the ordinary laws of algebra.

5. *To express $\Delta^m f(x)$ in terms of $f(x)$ and its successive values.*

$$\Delta^m f(x) = (E-1)^m f(x)$$

$$= \left[E^m - m E^{m-1} + \binom{m}{2} E^{m-2} - \ldots + (-1)^m\right] f(x)$$

$$= f(x+mh) - mf(x + \overline{m-1}h) + \binom{m}{2} f(x + \overline{m-2}h) - \ldots$$

$$+ (-1)^m f(x)\ldots\ldots(2).$$

Alternatively both the above formulas can be easily proved by the ordinary methods of induction.

Formula (1) also follows directly from the ordinary formula of Divided Differences (see Chapter VIII). This method has the advantage of showing directly the application of formula (1) to cases where m has a fractional or a negative value.

6. The above formulas are expressed in a form which applies in the most general way, i.e. when the interval of differencing is h and the leading term is $f(x)$. It is clear, however, that by altering the unit of measurement the formula will be simplified although the result is not affected. Similarly by changing the leading term (which process corresponds to shifting the "origin") so that the leading term is expressed as $f(0)$ a further simplification in form is made.

If, therefore, the interval of differencing becomes unity and the leading term can be represented by $f(0)$, the first formula can be written

$$f(n) = f(0) + n\Delta f(0) + \binom{n}{2}\Delta^2 f(0) + \ldots \quad \ldots\ldots(3).$$

An example will make this clear.

Having given the values of $f(10)$, $f(15)$, $f(20)$, etc. it is desired to express $f(17)$ in terms of $f(10)$ and its leading differences.

The original formula (1) gives the value of $f(10 + 1\cdot 4h)$, where $h = 5$, and therefore we write

$$f(10 + 1\cdot 4h) = f(10) + 1\cdot 4\Delta f(10) + \frac{(1\cdot 4)(\cdot 4)}{2}\Delta^2 f(10) + \ldots,$$

where Δ, Δ^2, ... are taken over the interval h.

But the same result is secured if the unit of measurement is changed from 1 to 5 and if at the same time $f(10)$ is made the initial term of the series, for then $f(10)$, $f(15)$, $f(20)$, ... can be written as $F(0)$, $F(1)$, $F(2)$, ... and the required value, viz. $f(17)$, becomes $F(1\cdot 4)$ which by formula (3) is equal to

$$F(0) + 1\cdot 4\Delta F(0) + \frac{(1\cdot 4)(\cdot 4)}{2}\Delta^2 F(0) + \ldots.$$

7. The above formulas are of general application if sufficient terms of the series are known, but it is convenient at this stage to consider the particular forms taken by the differences of certain special functions.

8. $f(x) = ax^n$,

$$\Delta f(x) = a(x+1)^n - ax^n = a\left[nx^{n-1} + \binom{n}{2}x^{n-2} + \ldots + 1\right].$$

The result of differencing has been, therefore, to change the term involving the highest power of x from ax^n to anx^{n-1} (thus reducing its degree in x).

Similarly a further process of differencing will reduce the degree of x to $n-2$ and the coefficient of the highest power of x will be an $(n-1)$. By repeating the process we arrive at the result that the nth difference of ax^n is independent of x and is equal to $a \cdot n!$. The $(n+1)$th difference is therefore zero.

Corollary. It follows that the nth difference of

$$ax^n + bx^{n-1} + cx^{n-2} + \dots + k$$

is constant and equal to $a \cdot n!$.

9. $$f(x) = x(x-1)(x-2)\dots(x-m+1).$$

This expression is usually denoted by $x^{(m)}$.

$$\Delta f(x) = (x+1)x(x-1)\dots(x-m+2) - x(x-1)(x-2)\dots(x-m+1)$$

$$= mx(x-1)\dots(x-m+2)$$

$$= mx^{(m-1)}.$$

Similarly $$\Delta^2 f(x) = m(m-1)x^{(m-2)}.$$

By repeating the process we arrive at the result

$$\Delta^m f(x) = m!,$$

which is otherwise obvious from the preceding article since $f(x)$ is of the mth degree in x.

10. $$f(x) = \frac{1}{x(x+1)(x+2)\dots(x+m-1)}.$$

Corresponding to the notation already used, this can be denoted by $x^{(-m)}$.

$$\Delta f(x) = \frac{1}{(x+1)(x+2)\dots(x+m)} - \frac{1}{x(x+1)(x+2)\dots(x+m-1)}$$

$$= \frac{-m}{x(x+1)(x+2)\dots(x+m)}$$

$$= -mx^{(-\overline{m+1})}.$$

Similarly $$\Delta^2 f(x) = m(m+1)x^{(-\overline{m+2})}$$

and so on.

11. $$f(x) = a^x,$$

$$\Delta f(x) = a^{x+1} - a^x$$

$$= a^x(a-1).$$

Whence $$\Delta^n f(x) = a^x(a-1)^n.$$

12. For many purposes it is convenient to have a table of the leading differences of the powers of the natural numbers. These can be represented as the differences of $[x^n]_{x=0}$ and are sometimes known as the "Differences of 0."

The following table gives a number of values of the first term and leading differences of $[\Delta^m x^n]_{x=0}$, which, for convenience, can be written as $\Delta^m 0^n$:

n	$f(0)$	Δ	Δ^2	Δ^3	Δ^4	Δ^5	Δ^6
1	0	1	0	—	—	—	—
2	0	1	2	0	—	—	—
3	0	1	6	6	0	—	—
4	0	1	14	36	24	0	—
5	0	1	30	150	240	120	0

13. A working formula for constructing a table such as the above by a continuous process may be obtained as follows:

$$\Delta^n f(x) = f(x+n) - nf(x+n-1) + \binom{n}{2} f(x+n-2) - \dots .$$

[See formula (2).]

Therefore, when $f(x) = x^m$,

$$\Delta^n x^m = (x+n)^m - n(x+n-1)^m + \binom{n}{2}(x+n-2)^m \dots ,$$

whence, putting $x = 0$,

$$\Delta^n 0^m = n^m - n(n-1)^m + \binom{n}{2}(n-2)^m - \dots$$

$$= n\left[n^{m-1} - (n-1)(n-1)^{m-1} + \binom{n-1}{2}(n-2)^{m-1} - \dots \right]$$

$$= n\left[(1+\overline{n-1})^{m-1} - (n-1)(1+\overline{n-2})^{m-1} \right.$$

$$\left. + \binom{n-1}{2}(1+\overline{n-3})^{m-1} - \dots \right]$$

$$= n[\Delta^{n-1} x^{m-1}]_{x=1} \quad \dots\dots\dots\dots\dots\dots\dots\dots\dots\dots\dots\dots\dots (4).$$

But
$$f(1) = f(0) + \Delta f(0),$$

and
$$\Delta^{n-1} f(1) = \Delta^{n-1} f(0) + \Delta^n f(0).$$

Therefore

$$[\Delta^{n-1} x^{m-1}]_{x=1} = [\Delta^{n-1} x^{m-1}]_{x=0} + [\Delta^n x^{m-1}]_{x=0}$$

$$= \Delta^{n-1} 0^{m-1} + \Delta^n 0^{m-1}.$$

Hence $\qquad \Delta^n 0^m = n\left[\Delta^{n-1}0^{m-1} + \Delta^n 0^{m-1}\right]$ ....(5).

It follows that the differences of $[x^m]_{x=0}$ can be constructed from those of $[x^{m-1}]_{x=0}$, and so on.

To take an example from the table given above,

$$\Delta^4 0^5 = 4\left[\Delta^3 0^4 + \Delta^4 0^4\right]$$
$$= 4\left[36 + 24\right] = 240.$$

14. By using the result given in § 9, it is possible to expand $f(x)$ in terms of $x^{(0)}$, $x^{(1)}$, $x^{(2)}$, ...

Let $\qquad f(x) = A_0 + A_1 x^{(1)} + A_2 x^{(2)} + A_3 x^{(3)} + \dots.$

Then, putting $x = 0$, we see that

$$f(0) = A_0.$$

Differencing both sides of the equation, we get

$$\Delta f(x) = A_1 + 2A_2 x^{(1)} + 3A_3 x^{(2)} + \dots.$$

Again putting $x = 0$, we find

$$\Delta f(0) = A_1.$$

By repeating the above processes, we obtain successively

$$\Delta^2 f(0) = 2!\, A_2, \quad \Delta^3 f(0) = 3!\, A_3, \dots \quad \Delta^n f(0) = n!\, A_n,$$

whence

$$A_0 = f(0), \quad A_1 = \Delta f(0), \quad A_2 = \frac{\Delta^2 f(0)}{2!}, \dots \quad A_n = \frac{\Delta^n f(0)}{n!},$$

and

$$f(x) = f(0) + x\Delta f(0) + \frac{x^2}{2!}\Delta^2 f(0) + \dots + \frac{x^n}{n!}\Delta^n f(0) + \dots \quad (6).$$

CHAPTER IV

FINITE DIFFERENCES. INTERPOLATION

1. The subject of interpolation is one of the most important in Finite Differences and may be enunciated as follows.

It frequently happens that we have given a number of values of $f(x)$ corresponding to different values of x, and we wish to find a value of the function for some other value of x. If the form of the function is known or can be deduced from the given values, the problem is, of course, simple, although in many cases it is more convenient to proceed by the methods of Finite Differences. But it is frequently the case, especially in actuarial work, that the function cannot be expressed, algebraically or otherwise, in any simple form, and resort must be had to other devices.

2. Looked at from the point of view of a problem in graphs, we may regard the given values of the function as representing a number of isolated points on a curve, and it is desired to plot a further point corresponding to a given value of the abscissa.

It follows that if the form of the function (i.e. the equation of the curve) is unknown, some assumption must be made as to the relationship between the different values. The formulas of finite differences assume that this relationship can be expressed in the form

$$y = a + bx + cx^2 + dx^3 + \dots + kx^{n-1}.$$

This assumes (see Chapter III, § 8) that all orders of differences higher than the $(n-1)$th vanish, but, as pointed out in Chapter II, § 4, this assumption can be made without introducing important errors in practically all cases where actuarial functions are involved.

3. The above equation contains n constants, and therefore n values of the function must be known if the values of the constants are to be determined. Conversely, if n values only are known and the methods of finite differences are to be applied, it must be assumed implicitly that all orders of differences higher than the $(n-1)$th vanish.

4. The most obvious method of procedure is to obtain the n equations given by the n values of the function and to find the values of the constants therefrom. The assumed form of the function is then completely determined and the value corresponding to any value of x can be obtained.

In the majority of cases, however, this is not the most simple method of working, for other devices can be adopted which will materially shorten the arithmetical work. It is important to note, however, that alternative formulas, in which the same values of the function are used, lead to identical results.

In some cases there is scope for the exercise of the ingenuity of the solver, but usually the problems fall into the main categories which are illustrated in the following examples.

5. *Example* 1. When n equidistant values of a function are given and it is required to find the value of some intermediate term or terms.

This can be done readily by the application of formula (1) of Chapter III, or by the simpler formula (3). From the given values the successive orders of differences are calculated, and the result is obtained by direct substitution.

Thus, taking the numbers living by the H^M table at ages 45, 50, 55, 60 and 65, it is required to find the value for age 57.

In conformance with formula (3) the given values can be denoted by $f(0), f(1), \ldots$, so that the required value is $f(2\cdot4)$. Then

$$f(2\cdot4) = f(0) + 2\cdot4\, \Delta f(0) + \frac{2\cdot4 \times 1\cdot4}{2}\, \Delta^2 f(0)$$
$$+ \frac{2\cdot4 \times 1\cdot4 \times \cdot4}{6}\, \Delta^3 f(0) + \frac{2\cdot4 \times 1\cdot4 \times \cdot4 \times -\cdot6}{24}\, \Delta^4 f(0).$$

The working is as follows:

x	$f(x)$	$\Delta f(x)$	$\Delta^2 f(x)$	$\Delta^3 f(x)$	$\Delta^4 f(x)$
0	77918	-5123	-1106	-389	$+75$
1	72795	-6229	-1495	-314	
2	66566	-7724	-1809		
3	58842	-9533			
4	49309				

From above:
$$f(2\cdot4) = 77918 + 2\cdot4\,(-5123) + 1\cdot68\,(-1106)$$
$$+ \cdot224\,(-389) - \cdot0336\,(+75)$$
$$= 77918 - 12295\cdot2 - 1858\cdot1 - 87\cdot1 - 2\cdot5$$
$$= 63675\cdot1.$$

The value given by the table is 63677.

The difference between the interpolated value and the true value is due to the fact that the interpolation curve, which is based on the assumption that all differences of higher order than the fourth vanish, represents only approximately the true function.

6. *Example* 2. When the values given and the value sought constitute a series of equidistant terms.

If there are n terms given of which $n-1$ are known, then, as explained in § 3, it must be assumed that the $(n-1)$th order of differences is zero.

Thus, using formula (2) of Chapter III, we have

$$\Delta^{n-1} f(0) = 0 = f(n-1) - (n-1)f(n-2) + \binom{n-1}{2} f(n-3) - \dots$$
$$+ (-1)^{n-1} f(0).$$

In this equation there is only one unknown quantity and its value can, therefore, be readily obtained.

For example, if

$$f(0) = \log 3{\cdot}50 = {\cdot}54407,$$
$$f(1) = \log 3{\cdot}51 = {\cdot}54531,$$
$$f(2) = \log 3{\cdot}52 = {\cdot}54654,$$
$$f(4) = \log 3{\cdot}54 = {\cdot}54900,$$

and it is required to find $\log 3{\cdot}53$, i.e. $f(3)$.

From above:

$$\Delta^4 f(0) = 0 = f(4) - 4f(3) + 6f(2) - 4f(1) + f(0),$$

whence
$$f(3) = \frac{f(4) + 6f(2) - 4f(1) + f(0)}{4}$$
$$= {\cdot}54777,$$

which agrees with the true value to five decimal places.

7. *Example* 3. If more than one term is missing from the complete series, a somewhat similar process may be followed. Thus, if two terms are missing, only $(n-2)$ terms are known and the $(n-2)$th order of differences must be assumed to vanish. It is then possible to construct two equations:

$$\Delta^{n-2} f(0) = f(n-2) - (n-2) f(n-3) + \dots + (-1)^{n-2} f(0) = 0,$$
$$\Delta^{n-2} f(1) = f(n-1) - (n-2) f(n-2) + \dots + (-1)^{n-2} f(1) = 0.$$

From these equations, the values of the two unknowns can be calculated.

Similarly if a larger number of terms is missing, the method can be extended.

8. *Example* 4. If several equidistant values are given, together with one isolated term.

For instance, if three values $f(0)$, $f(1)$ and $f(2)$ are given, together with a further value $f(h)$. Having four values of the function it must be assumed that the fourth order of differences is zero and it remains to find the values of the other three leading differences. The first two leading differences are obtained at once by differencing the first three terms of the series, and the value of the third difference is then given by the equation

$$f(h) = f(0) + h\Delta f(0) + \binom{h}{2} \Delta^2 f(0) + \binom{h}{3} \Delta^3 f(0).$$

For example, taking the numbers living by the H^M table at ages 45, 46, 47 and 50, it is required to find values for ages 48 and 49.

$$
\begin{array}{lll}
 & \Delta & \Delta^2 \\
f(0) = 77918 & -954 & -32 \\
f(1) = 76964 & -986 & \\
f(2) = 75978 & & \\
f(5) = 72795 & & \\
\end{array}
$$

$$f(5) = f(0) + 5\Delta f(0) + 10\Delta^2 f(0) + 10\Delta^3 f(0),$$

$$\Delta^3 f(0) = \frac{f(5) - [f(0) + 5\Delta f(0) + 10\Delta^2 f(0)]}{10}$$

$$= \frac{72795 - [77918 - 4770 - 320]}{10}$$

$$= -3\cdot3.$$

The table is then completed by addition. Thus:

Age x	$f(x)$	Δ	Δ^2	Δ^3
45	77918	− 954	− 32	− 3·3
46	76964	− 986	− 35·3	− 3·3
47	75978	− 1021·3	− 38·6	− 3·3
48	74956·7	− 1059·9	− 41·9	
49	73896·8	− 1101·8		
50	72795·0			

The work is checked by the reproduction of the value for age 50.

The tabular values for ages 48 and 49 are 74957 and 73896 respectively.

Values precisely the same as those obtained above would have been given if the two missing terms had been inserted by the method described in Example 3. It is instructive to confirm this by actual calculation and to compare the two methods of procedure.

9. Example 5. Subdivision of Intervals.

This problem arises when a series of equidistant terms of a series is given (usually every fifth term or every tenth term) and it is desired to find by interpolation the values of all the intermediate terms.

The simplest method of procedure is to calculate from the given values the differences corresponding to the individual terms of the series (the *subdivided differences*) and thence to construct the table by summation. The calculation is checked by the reproduction of the values of the original terms.

Thus assume that the given terms are $f(0)$, $f(1)$, ... $f(5)$ and it is desired to complete the series $f(0)$, $f(\frac{1}{5})$, $f(\frac{2}{5})$, etc. It is convenient to adopt the notation

$$f(1) - f(0) = \Delta f(0),$$

and
$$f(\tfrac{1}{5}) - f(0) = \delta f(0).$$

The problem then becomes to express $\delta f(0)$, $\delta^2 f(0)$, ... in terms of $\Delta f(0)$, $\Delta^2 f(0)$, ...

Writing $f(1)$, $f(2)$, ... in terms of the subdivided differences,

$$
\begin{aligned}
f(0) &= f(0) \\
f(1) &= f(0) + 5\delta f(0) + 10\delta^2 f(0) + 10\delta^3 f(0) + 5\delta^4 f(0) + \delta^5 f(0) \\
f(2) &= f(0) + 10\delta f(0) + 45\delta^2 f(0) + 120\delta^3 f(0) + 210\delta^4 f(0) + 252\delta^5 f(0) \\
f(3) &= f(0) + 15\delta f(0) + 105\delta^2 f(0) + 455\delta^3 f(0) + 1365\delta^4 f(0) + 3003\delta^5 f(0) \\
f(4) &= f(0) + 20\delta f(0) + 190\delta^2 f(0) + 1140\delta^3 f(0) + 4845\delta^4 f(0) + 15504\delta^5 f(0) \\
f(5) &= f(0) + 25\delta f(0) + 300\delta^2 f(0) + 2300\delta^3 f(0) + 12650\delta^4 f(0) + 53130\delta^5 f(0)
\end{aligned}
$$

Differencing successively both sides of the equation, we have

$$
\begin{aligned}
\Delta f(0) &= 5\delta f(0) + 10\delta^2 f(0) + 10\delta^3 f(0) + 5\delta^4 f(0) + \delta^5 f(0) \\
\Delta f(1) &= 5\delta f(0) + 35\delta^2 f(0) + 110\delta^3 f(0) + 205\delta^4 f(0) + 251\delta^5 f(0) \\
\Delta f(2) &= 5\delta f(0) + 60\delta^2 f(0) + 335\delta^3 f(0) + 1155\delta^4 f(0) + 2751\delta^5 f(0) \\
\Delta f(3) &= 5\delta f(0) + 85\delta^2 f(0) + 685\delta^3 f(0) + 3480\delta^4 f(0) + 12501\delta^5 f(0) \\
\Delta f(4) &= 5\delta f(0) + 110\delta^2 f(0) + 1160\delta^3 f(0) + 7805\delta^4 f(0) + 37626\delta^5 f(0)
\end{aligned}
$$

$$
\begin{aligned}
\Delta^2 f(0) &= 25\delta^2 f(0) + 100\delta^3 f(0) + 200\delta^4 f(0) + 250\delta^5 f(0) \\
\Delta^2 f(1) &= 25\delta^2 f(0) + 225\delta^3 f(0) + 950\delta^4 f(0) + 2500\delta^5 f(0) \\
\Delta^2 f(2) &= 25\delta^2 f(0) + 350\delta^3 f(0) + 2325\delta^4 f(0) + 9750\delta^5 f(0) \\
\Delta^2 f(3) &= 25\delta^2 f(0) + 475\delta^3 f(0) + 4325\delta^4 f(0) + 25125\delta^5 f(0)
\end{aligned}
$$

$$
\begin{aligned}
\Delta^3 f(0) &= 125\delta^3 f(0) + 750\delta^4 f(0) + 2250\delta^5 f(0) \\
\Delta^3 f(1) &= 125\delta^3 f(0) + 1375\delta^4 f(0) + 7250\delta^5 f(0) \\
\Delta^3 f(2) &= 125\delta^3 f(0) + 2000\delta^4 f(0) + 15375\delta^5 f(0)
\end{aligned}
$$

$$
\begin{aligned}
\Delta^4 f(0) &= 625\delta^4 f(0) + 5000\delta^5 f(0) \\
\Delta^4 f(1) &= 625\delta^4 f(0) + 8125\delta^5 f(0)
\end{aligned}
$$

$$\Delta^5 f(0) = 3125\delta^5 f(0)$$

Whence the values of $\delta f(0)$, $\delta^2 f(0)$, ... $\delta^5 f(0)$ can readily be obtained.

10. Alternatively the formulas for δ, δ^2, ... can easily be written down by using the method of Separation of Symbols.

Thus $\qquad (1+\delta)^5 f(x) = (1+\Delta) f(x)$.

Therefore $\quad (1+\delta) f(x) = (1+\Delta)^{\frac{1}{5}} f(x)$,

and $\qquad \delta f(x) = [(1+\Delta)^{\frac{1}{5}} - 1] f(x)$

$\qquad\qquad = [\cdot 2\Delta - \cdot 08\Delta^2 + \cdot 048\Delta^3 \dots] f(x)$.

Hence $\qquad \delta^2 f(x) = [\cdot 2\Delta - \cdot 08\Delta^2 + \cdot 048\Delta^3 \dots]^2 f(x)$

$\qquad\qquad = [\cdot 04\Delta^2 - \cdot 032\Delta^3 + \cdot 0256\Delta^4 \dots] f(x)$

and so on.

For convenience the coefficients of Δ, Δ^2, ... occurring in the values of δ, δ^2, ... are given, for the intervals 5 and 10, in the following tables.

Subdivision into 5 intervals

Value of	Coefficient of				
	Δ	Δ^2	Δ^3	Δ^4	Δ^5
δ	$+\cdot 2$	$-\cdot 08$	$+\cdot 048$	$-\cdot 0336$	$+\cdot 025536$
δ^2		$+\cdot 04$	$-\cdot 032$	$+\cdot 0256$	$-\cdot 02112$
δ^3			$+\cdot 008$	$-\cdot 0096$	$+\cdot 00960$
δ^4				$+\cdot 0016$	$-\cdot 00256$
δ^5					$+\cdot 00032$

Subdivision into 10 intervals

Value of	Coefficient of				
	Δ	Δ^2	Δ^3	Δ^4	Δ^5
δ	$+\cdot 1$	$-\cdot 045$	$+\cdot 0285$	$-\cdot 0206625$	$+\cdot 01611675$
δ^2		$+\cdot 01$	$-\cdot 009$	$+\cdot 007725$	$-\cdot 0066975$
δ^3			$+\cdot 001$	$-\cdot 00135$	$+\cdot 0014625$
δ^4				$+\cdot 0001$	$-\cdot 00018$
δ^5					$+\cdot 00001$

11. The following example gives an illustration of the method of working.

Given the present values, at 3 per cent. interest, of an annuity of 1 per annum for 20, 25, ... 45 years, it is required to find the intervening values.

We have

x	$f(x)$	Δ	Δ^2	Δ^3	Δ^4	Δ^5
20	14·8775	2·5356	− ·3483	·0478	− ·0065	·0007
25	17·4131	2·1873	− ·3005	·0413	− ·0058	
30	19·6004	1·8868	− ·2592	·0355		
35	21·4872	1·6276	− ·2237			
40	23·1148	1·4039				
45	24·5187					

Applying the factors given in the former of the above tables, we have

$$\delta f(20) = [\cdot 2\Delta - \cdot 08\Delta^2 + \cdot 048\Delta^3 - \cdot 0336\Delta^4 + \cdot 025536\Delta^5]f(20)$$

$$= \cdot 2 \times 2\cdot 5356 + \cdot 08 \times \cdot 3483 + \cdot 048 \times \cdot 0478 + \cdot 0336 \times \cdot 0065$$
$$+ \cdot 025536 \times \cdot 0007$$

$$= \cdot 5375146752.$$

Similarly

$$\delta^2 = - \cdot 015642784, \qquad \delta^4 = - \cdot 000012192,$$
$$\delta^3 = \cdot 000451520, \qquad \delta^5 = \cdot 000000224.$$

The table is then constructed by addition from these leading differences as shown below.

It is necessary to consider how many decimal places should be retained in the working. This depends, in the first place, on the degree of accuracy desired in the result. Thus if four decimal places are required in $f(x)$, our result must be given to at least one place more. Further, the range of the formula is 25 terms, and in the final term the values of $\delta, \delta^2, \dots \delta^5$ are multiplied respectively by $\binom{25}{1}, \binom{25}{2}, \dots \binom{25}{5}$, which are respectively equal to 25, 300, 2300, 12650, 53130. In view of the magnitude of these coefficients, we shall need to retain at least six decimal places more in the value of δ^5 than are required in the final value of $f(x)$. Since the coefficients of the lower orders of differences are smaller than 53130, a correspondingly smaller number of decimal places can be retained. In practice, however, there is little to be gained by cutting down, unless only a rough result is required.

The working of the first five terms in the example is shown below. It will be noticed that the accuracy of the work up to this stage is checked by the exact reproduction of the value of $f(25)$. The interpolated values agree exactly with the true values to four places of decimals.

x	$f(x)$	δ	δ^2	δ^3	δ^4	δ^5
20	14·8775	·5375147	− ·01564278	·000451520	− ·000012192	·000000224
21	15·415015	·5218719	1519126	439328	11968	224
22	15·936887	·5066806	1475193	427360	11744	224
23	16·443568	·4919287	1432457	415616	11520	224
24	16·935497	·4776041	1390895	404096	11296	224
25	17·413101	·4636951	1350485	392800	11072	224

12. *Example 6. Lagrange's Theorem.*

We have now to consider the construction of an interpolation formula which will apply when the given terms of the series are not equidistant.

Let n values of the function be given, namely

$$f(a), f(b), f(c), \ldots f(n).$$

Then the function must be assumed to be a parabolic function of x of degree $(n-1)$. (See § 3.) Assume therefore that the function can be represented as

$$\begin{aligned} f(x) = \quad & A\,(x-b)(x-c)\ldots(x-n) \\ & + B\,(x-a)(x-c)\ldots(x-n) \\ & + C(x-a)(x-b)\ldots(x-n) \\ & + \text{etc.,} \end{aligned}$$

there being n terms in all, each composed of $(n-1)$ factors multiplied by a constant, the values of the constants having yet to be determined. It is clear that the right-hand side of the equation is of degree $(n-1)$.

To find the values of the constants we proceed as follows:

Put $$x = a.$$

Then $$f(a) = A\,(a-b)(a-c)\ldots(a-n).$$

Therefore $$A = \frac{f(a)}{(a-b)(a-c)\ldots(a-n)}.$$

Similarly $$B = \frac{f(b)}{(b-a)(b-c)\ldots(b-n)},$$

and so on.

Substituting these values of $A, B, \ldots$ in the original equation we have

$$f(x) = f(a)\frac{(x-b)(x-c)\ldots(x-n)}{(a-b)(a-c)\ldots(a-n)} + f(b)\frac{(x-a)(x-c)\ldots(x-n)}{(b-a)(b-c)\ldots(b-n)}$$

$$+ \ldots + f(n)\frac{(x-a)(x-b)(x-c)\ldots}{(n-a)(n-b)(n-c)\ldots} \quad \ldots(1).$$

By an obvious transformation, the formula can be put in a somewhat simpler form for calculations, namely

$$\frac{f(x)}{(x-a)(x-b)\ldots(x-n)} = \frac{f(a)}{(x-a)(a-b)(a-c)\ldots(a-n)}$$

$$+ \frac{f(b)}{(b-a)(x-b)\ldots(b-n)} + \ldots + \frac{f(n)}{(n-a)(n-b)(n-c)\ldots(x-n)}$$

$$\ldots\ldots\ldots(2).$$

In memorising the formula it should be noted that the denominators are made up of the product of the algebraic differences of the values of the variable, the term $(a-a)$ being replaced by $(x-a)$ and so on.

13. The formula is somewhat laborious to apply, and careful attention to signs is required, but it is convenient to use where only one or two unknown values of the function are required. Since the assumptions underlying it are precisely similar to those previously explained, its use in any particular case will give identical results with those which can be obtained by the use of the ordinary methods of Finite Differences where a sufficiently high order of differences has been taken into account.

To illustrate this point and to provide an example of the use of the formula, we will calculate by Lagrange's formula the value for age 49 in Example 4. In this case we have

$$f(0) = 77918, \quad f(1) = 76964, \quad f(2) = 75978, \quad f(5) = 72795,$$

and it is required to find the value of $f(4)$.

We have accordingly

$$\frac{f(4)}{(4-0)(4-1)(4-2)(4-5)} = \frac{f(0)}{(4-0)(0-1)(0-2)(0-5)}$$

$$+ \frac{f(1)}{(1-0)(4-1)(1-2)(1-5)} + \frac{f(2)}{(2-0)(2-1)(4-2)(2-5)}$$

$$+ \frac{f(5)}{(5-0)(5-1)(5-2)(4-5)},$$

or, $-\frac{1}{24}f(4) = -\frac{1}{40}f(0) + \frac{1}{12}f(1) - \frac{1}{12}f(2) - \frac{1}{80}f(5).$

Whence we find $f(4) = 73896\cdot8$, as before.

It should be noted, as a check on the formula, that the sum of the coefficients of the terms on the right-hand side of the equation must equal the coefficient of the term on the left-hand side of the equation.

14. Problems of interpolation between terms at unequal intervals can also be dealt with in a simple way by the formulas of Divided Differences (see Chapter VIII).

CHAPTER V

FINITE DIFFERENCES. CENTRAL DIFFERENCES

1. It has already been stated that in interpolating between given values of a function the form of the expression connecting these values is assumed to be parabolic, and that this assumption is usually only an approximation to the truth. It remains therefore to be considered by what methods the best result can be obtained by the processes of Finite Differences.

2. In developing the formulas of this chapter, it will be assumed that a number of equidistant values of the function are given. Let us assume further that it is desired to interpolate a value $f(x)$ intermediate between $f(0)$ and $f(1)$. It is clear that our knowledge of the shape of the curve on which the points lie is increased if we are given values of the function lying on both sides of $f(0)$, and that generally the best value of $f(x)$ will be obtained, if a limited number of terms is to be used, when the required value occupies as nearly as possible a central position in regard to the terms used in the interpolation.

The formulas of Central Differences are designed to give effect to these considerations.

3. The more familiar formulas of Central Differences are as follows:

STIRLING'S:

$$f(x) = f(0) + x\,\frac{\Delta f(0) + \Delta f(-1)}{2} + \frac{x^2}{2}\Delta^2 f(-1)$$

$$+ \frac{x(x^2-1)}{3!}\,\frac{\Delta^3 f(-1) + \Delta^3 f(-2)}{2} + \frac{x^2(x^2-1)}{4!}\Delta^4 f(-2)$$

$$+ \frac{x(x^2-1)(x^2-4)}{5!}\,\frac{\Delta^5 f(-2) + \Delta^5 f(-3)}{2}$$

$$+ \frac{x^2(x^2-1)(x^2-4)}{6!}\Delta^6 f(-3) + \dots \quad\dots\dots\dots\dots(1).$$

BESSEL'S:

$$f(x) = \frac{f(0) + f(1)}{2} + (x - \tfrac{1}{2}) \Delta f(0)$$

$$+ \frac{x(x-1)}{2!} \frac{\Delta^2 f(-1) + \Delta^2 f(0)}{2} + \frac{(x - \tfrac{1}{2}) x (x-1)}{3!} \Delta^3 f(-1)$$

$$+ \frac{(x+1) x (x-1)(x-2)}{4!} \frac{\Delta^4 f(-1) + \Delta^4 f(-2)}{2}$$

$$+ \frac{(x - \tfrac{1}{2})(x+1) x (x-1)(x-2)}{5!} \Delta^5 f(-2)$$

$$+ \frac{(x+2)(x+1) x (x-1)(x-2)(x-3)}{6!} \frac{\Delta^6 f(-2) + \Delta^6 f(-3)}{2} + \dots$$

$$\dots\dots\dots(2).$$

GAUSS':

$$f(x) = f(0) + x \Delta f(0) + \frac{x(x-1)}{2!} \Delta^2 f(-1) + \frac{(x+1) x (x-1)}{3!} \Delta^3 f(-1)$$

$$+ \frac{(x+1) x (x-1)(x-2)}{4!} \Delta^4 f(-2)$$

$$+ \frac{(x+2)(x+1) x (x-1)(x-2)}{5!} \Delta^5 f(-2) + \dots \ \dots(3).$$

EVERETT'S:

$$f(x) = x f(1) + \frac{x(x^2-1)}{3!} \Delta^2 f(0) + \frac{x(x^2-1)(x^2-4)}{5!} \Delta^4 f(-1)$$

$$+ \frac{x(x^2-1)(x^2-4)(x^2-9)}{7!} \Delta^6 f(-2) + \dots$$

$$+ y f(0) + \frac{y(y^2-1)}{3!} \Delta^2 f(-1) + \frac{y(y^2-1)(y^2-4)}{5!} \Delta^4 f(-2)$$

$$+ \frac{y(y^2-1)(y^2-4)(y^2-9)}{7!} \Delta^6 f(-3) + \dots \ \dots\dots\dots(4).$$

[where $y = 1 - x$].

4. These formulas can be obtained in various ways from the ordinary formulas of advancing differences. Once, however, the scheme of differences entering into a formula is settled, the co-efficients can readily be calculated by the method of Separation of Symbols. An example may be given of the demonstration of Gauss' formula by this method.

Example 1.

To express $f(x)$ in terms of $f(0)$, $\Delta f(0)$, $\Delta^2 f(-1)$, $\Delta^3 f(-1)$, ...

Let $\quad f(x) = A_0 f(0) + A_1 \Delta f(0) + A_2 \Delta^2 f(-1) + ...$

Then, since

$$\Delta^2 f(-1) = \frac{\Delta^2}{1+\Delta} f(0); \quad \Delta^3 f(-1) = \frac{\Delta^3}{1+\Delta} f(0); \text{ etc.,}$$

$$(1+\Delta)^x = A_0 + A_1 \Delta + A_2 \frac{\Delta^2}{1+\Delta} + A_3 \frac{\Delta^3}{1+\Delta} + \cdots$$

$$+ A_{2r-1} \frac{\Delta^{2r-1}}{(1+\Delta)^{r-1}} + A_{2r} \frac{\Delta^{2r}}{(1+\Delta)^r} + \cdots.$$

Multiplying up by $(1+\Delta)^{r-1}$, and equating coefficients of Δ^{2r-1},

$$A_{2r-1} = \frac{(r+x-1)(r+x-2)\ldots(x-r+1)}{(2r-1)!}.$$

And, multiplying up by $(1+\Delta)^r$, and equating coefficients of Δ^{2r},

$$A_{2r-1} + A_{2r} = \frac{(r+x)(r+x-1)\ldots(x-r+1)}{2r!}.$$

Hence, by subtraction,

$$A_{2r} = \frac{(r+x-1)(r+x-2)\ldots(x-r)}{2r!}.$$

Therefore $f(x) = f(0) + x\Delta f(0)$

$$+ \frac{x(x-1)}{2!} \Delta^2 f(-1) + \frac{(x+1)x(x-1)}{3!} \Delta^3 f(-1) + \cdots.$$

The other formulas should be proved, in a similar way, as exercises by the student*.

5. The formulas of central differences, although in a different form, are intimately associated with those of advancing differences. For example, if an interpolated value is calculated by using the first three terms of Stirling's formula, it is obvious that the values

* See *J. I. A.* Vol. 50, pp. 28–33.

of $f(-1)$, $f(0)$ and $f(1)$ are brought into the calculation. It is easy to show that the result is identical with that obtained by using the first three terms of the advancing difference formula starting with the term $f(-1)$.

It may be observed that the first two terms of Stirling's formula also involve three values of the function; the third term merely introduces the correction necessary to make the formula true to the order of differences (i.e. the second) implied by the use of three terms of the series. Thus, as the $(2r)$th and the $(2r+1)$th terms of Stirling's formula both involve the use of $(2r+1)$ values of the function, there is ordinarily little advantage in using the extra $(2r+1)$th term in any calculation.

Similarly in Bessel's formula no material increase in precision is gained by using $2r$ terms rather than $2r-1$ terms.

Gauss' and Everett's formulas are each true to the order of differences involved and for general use they would appear to be the best of those propounded.

6. In view of the remarks at the beginning of the foregoing article, it may well be asked what are the advantages of central difference formulas, as compared with advancing difference formulas so chosen as to make the interpolated term as nearly as possible the central term of those employed. It may at once be said that the theoretical advantages are small but that the practical advantages may be considerable. Thus if it be desired to introduce further terms of the original series into the calculation, the original calculations relating to the central difference formulas hold good, and the values of fresh terms of the formula can be calculated until the desired degree of approximation is attained. If however an advancing difference formula is used, the introduction of fresh terms of the original series, while retaining the interpolated term in a central position, necessitates the changing of the origin and the recalculation of all the terms of the formula. An example will make this point clear.

7. *Example* 2. Required to interpolate the value of a unit accumulated for 17 years with compound interest at 5 per cent. per annum, having given the values for 0, 5, 10,...30 years.

For central difference formulas we must take our origin at 15 years, and we will take 5 years as the unit. Thus we get the following scheme:

No. of years	x	$f(x)$	Δ	Δ^2	Δ^3	Δ^4	Δ^5
0	−3	1·	·27628	·07633	·02110	·00580	·00165
5	−2	1·27628	·35261	·09743	·02690	·00745	·00206
10	−1	1·62889	·45004	·12433	·03435	·00951	
15	0	2·07893	·57437	·15868	·04386		
20	1	2·65330	·73305	·20254			
25	2	3·38635	·93559				
30	3	4·32194					

As the unit of time is 5 years, the required value is represented by $f(\cdot 4)$.

Central Differences. We will use Gauss' formula, i.e.

$$f(x) = f(0) + x\Delta f(0)$$

$$+ \frac{x(x-1)}{2!}\Delta^2 f(-1) + \frac{(x+1)x(x-1)}{3!}\Delta^3 f(-1) + \dots$$

The successive terms, with the corresponding values of $f(\cdot 4)$, are

$$f(0) = 2\cdot07893, \text{1st approx.} = 2\cdot07893$$

$$\cdot 4\Delta f(0) = \cdot22975, \text{2nd } \text{„} = 2\cdot30868$$

$$\frac{\cdot 4 \times -\cdot 6}{2}\Delta^2 f(-1) = -\cdot01492, \text{3rd } \text{„} = 2\cdot29376$$

$$\frac{1\cdot4 \times \cdot4 \times -\cdot6}{6}\Delta^3 f(-1) = -\cdot00192, \text{4th } \text{„} = 2\cdot29184$$

$$\frac{1\cdot4 \times \cdot4 \times -\cdot6 \times -1\cdot6}{24}\Delta^4 f(-2) = \cdot00017, \text{5th } \text{„} = 2\cdot29201$$

$$\frac{2\cdot4 \times 1\cdot4 \times \cdot4 \times -\cdot6 \times -1\cdot6}{120}\Delta^5 f(-2) = \cdot00002, \text{6th } \text{„} = 2\cdot29203$$

It is clear that no further terms would affect the calculated value. The true value is 2·29202.

Advancing Differences.

1st approximation $\qquad\qquad$ $f(0)$ $\qquad\qquad\qquad$ $= 2 \cdot 07893,$

2nd approximation $\qquad$ $f(0) + \cdot 4 \Delta f(0)$ $\qquad\qquad$ $= 2 \cdot 30868,$

3rd approximation

$$f(-1) + 1 \cdot 4 \Delta f(-1) + \frac{1 \cdot 4 \times \cdot 4}{2} \Delta^2 f(-1) \quad = 2 \cdot 29376,$$

4th approximation

$$f(-1) + 1 \cdot 4 \Delta f(-1) + \frac{1 \cdot 4 \times \cdot 4}{2} \Delta^2 f(-1)$$

$$+ \frac{1 \cdot 4 \times \cdot 4 \times - \cdot 6}{6} \Delta^3 f(-1) = 2 \cdot 29184,$$

5th approximation

$$f(-2) + 2 \cdot 4 \Delta f(-2) + \frac{2 \cdot 4 \times 1 \cdot 4}{2} \Delta^2 f(-2)$$

$$+ \frac{2 \cdot 4 \times 1 \cdot 4 \times \cdot 4}{6} \Delta^3 f(-2)$$

$$+ \frac{2 \cdot 4 \times 1 \cdot 4 \times \cdot 4 \times - \cdot 6}{24} \Delta^4 f(-2) = 2 \cdot 29200,$$

6th approximation

(5th approximation) $+ \dfrac{2 \cdot 4 \times 1 \cdot 4 \times \cdot 4 \times - \cdot 6 \times - 1 \cdot 6}{120} \Delta^5 f(-2) = 2 \cdot 29202.$

It will be observed that in proceeding to the 3rd and 5th approximations using advancing differences every term in the formula has to be recalculated, whereas, in the application of the central difference formula, terms already calculated hold good whatever be the degree of approximation.

It should be noted, however, that both formulas give mathematically the same results, the difference of a unit in the final figure being due to the use of only five places of decimals throughout.

8. As regards other practical points, it may be observed that the numerical coefficients in the central difference formulas are smaller than those in the advancing difference formulas (see Example 2).

Other advantages arise in special cases. Thus Bessel's formula can conveniently be applied for the bisection of an interval, since the alternate terms vanish, giving

$$f(\tfrac{1}{2}) = \frac{f(0) + f(1)}{2} - \frac{1}{8} \frac{\Delta^2 f(-1) + \Delta^2 f(0)}{2}$$
$$+ \frac{3}{128} \frac{\Delta^4 f(-2) + \Delta^4 f(-1)}{2} + \dots \quad (5).$$

Everett's formula gives the same value.

9. It should be noted as regards Everett's formula, that in calculating a series of values the work is nearly halved since it will be found that terms in the formula can be made to do duty twice, "x" terms reappearing in the calculation as "y" terms.

This will be seen at once, for,

$$f(x) = x f(1) + \frac{x(x^2 - 1)}{3!} \Delta^2 f(0) + \frac{x(x^2 - 1)(x^2 - 4)}{5!} \Delta^4 f(-1) + \dots$$
$$+ y f(0) + \frac{y(y^2 - 1)}{3!} \Delta^2 f(-1) + \frac{y(y^2 - 1)(y^2 - 4)}{5!} \Delta^4 f(-2) + \dots$$

and

$$f(1 + y) = y f(2) + \frac{y(y^2 - 1)}{3!} \Delta^2 f(1) + \frac{y(y^2 - 1)(y^2 - 4)}{5!} \Delta^4 f(0) + \dots$$
$$+ x f(1) + \frac{x(x^2 - 1)}{3!} \Delta^2 f(0) + \frac{x(x^2 - 1)(x^2 - 4)}{5!} \Delta^4 f(-1) + \dots,$$

the last line being identical with the first. Thus, if we are inserting terms in a series by subdividing the interval into five equal parts, $x = \cdot 2, \cdot 4, \dots$ and $y = \cdot 8, \cdot 6, \dots$. Therefore half of the terms used in the calculation of $f(\cdot 2)$ can be made to do duty in the calculation of $f(1\cdot 8)$, and similarly for the other terms.

10. An example will indicate the method of working.

Example 3. Using Everett's formula, interpolate the missing terms in the following series, between $f(40)$ and $f(50)$.

x	$f(x)$	Δ	Δ^2	Δ^3	Δ^4
30	771	91	48	36	5
35	862	139	84	41	37
40	1001	223	125	78	28
45	1224	348	203	106	
50	1572	551	309		
55	2123	860			
60	2983				

The coefficients of the several terms in Everett's formula are

·2	− ·032	·006336
·4	− ·056	·010752
·6	− ·064	·011648
·8	− ·048	·008064

The work may be arranged in tabular form:

x	$xf(1)$	$\dfrac{x(x^2-1)}{3!}\Delta^2 f(0)$	$\dfrac{x(x^2-1)(x^2-4)}{5!}\Delta^4 f(-1)$	Sum of first three terms (2) + (3) + (4)	Sum of second three terms	Interpolated result (5) + (6)
(1)	(2)	(3)	(4)	(5)	(6)	(7)
·2	200·2	− 2·6	0·0	197·6		
·4	400·4	− 4·7	0·1	395·8		
·6	600·6	− 5·4	0·1	595·3		
·8	800·8	− 4·0	0·0	796·8		
·2	244·8	− 4·0	0·2	241·0	796·8	1037·8
·4	489·6	− 7·0	0·4	483·0	595·3	1078·3
·6	734·4	− 8·0	0·4	726·8	395·8	1122·6
·8	979·2	− 6·0	0·3	973·5	197·6	1171·1
·2	314·4	− 6·5	0·2	308·1	973·5	1281·6
·4	628·8	−11·4	0·3	617·7	726·8	1344·5
·6	943·2	−13·0	0·3	930·5	483·0	1413·5
·8	1257·6	− 9·7	0·2	1248·1	241·0	1489·1

Columns (2), (3) and (4), which represent the first three terms of the formula, are obtained by ordinary multiplication. Column (5) gives the sum of these terms. From what has been said above, it is clear that column (6), which represents the second set of three terms of the formula to fourth central differences, is obtained by writing down, in reverse order, the values of column (5) applicable to the previous group of terms. The addition of columns (5) and (6) then gives the desired result.

The given values of $f(x)$ have been taken from the tabulated values of the probability of dying in a given year of age according to the H^M mortality table, multiplied by 10^5.

The tabular values for the interpolated terms are 1038, 1081, 1122, 1172, 1281, 1345, 1415, 1490. The small differences between these values and the interpolated values are due to the fact that the H^M table was constructed by means of a mathematical formula which is only approximately represented by Everett's formula.

11. Another method of applying the principles of central differences is to express the required function in terms of known values of the function among which it occupies a central position. This can conveniently be done by Lagrange's formula. The formulas are of two types according as the number of terms involved is odd or even. Thus we have by Lagrange:

Number of terms $2n + 1$.

3-*term formula,*

$$\frac{f(x)}{x(x^2-1)} = \frac{f(-1)}{2(x+1)} - \frac{f(0)}{x} + \frac{f(1)}{2(x-1)} \quad \ldots\ldots(6).$$

5-*term formula,*

$$\frac{f(x)}{x(x^2-1)(x^2-4)} = \frac{f(-2)}{24(x+2)} - \frac{f(-1)}{6(x+1)} + \frac{f(0)}{4x} - \frac{f(1)}{6(x-1)} + \frac{f(2)}{24(x-2)}$$
$$\ldots\ldots(7).$$

7-*term formula,*

$$\frac{f(x)}{x(x^2-1)(x^2-4)(x^2-9)} = \frac{f(-3)}{720(x+3)} - \frac{f(-2)}{120(x+2)} + \frac{f(-1)}{48(x+1)}$$
$$- \frac{f(0)}{36x} + \frac{f(1)}{48(x-1)} - \frac{f(2)}{120(x-2)} + \frac{f(3)}{720(x-3)} \quad \ldots\ldots(8).$$

Number of terms $2n$.

4-*term formula,*

$$\frac{f(x)}{(x^2-\frac{1}{4})(x^2-\frac{9}{4})} = -\frac{f(-\frac{3}{2})}{6(x+\frac{3}{2})} + \frac{f(-\frac{1}{2})}{2(x+\frac{1}{2})} - \frac{f(\frac{1}{2})}{2(x-\frac{1}{2})} + \frac{f(\frac{3}{2})}{6(x-\frac{3}{2})}$$
$$\ldots\ldots(9).$$

6-*term formula,*

$$\frac{f(x)}{(x^2-\frac{1}{4})(x^2-\frac{9}{4})(x^2-\frac{25}{4})} = -\frac{f(-\frac{5}{2})}{120(x+\frac{5}{2})} + \frac{f(-\frac{3}{2})}{24(x+\frac{3}{2})}$$
$$- \frac{f(-\frac{1}{2})}{12(x+\frac{1}{2})} + \frac{f(\frac{1}{2})}{12(x-\frac{1}{2})} - \frac{f(\frac{3}{2})}{24(x-\frac{3}{2})} + \frac{f(\frac{5}{2})}{120(x-\frac{5}{2})} \quad \ldots(10).$$

12. These formulas, of course, yield identically the same results as other central difference formulas embracing the same terms. To illustrate this we will recalculate the value of $f(\cdot4)$ in the example given in § 7.

Example 4. See Example 2. Seven terms are given, the formula will therefore be

$$\frac{f(\cdot 4)}{\cdot 4\,(\cdot 16-1)(\cdot 16-4)(\cdot 16-9)} = \frac{f(-3)}{720\times 3\cdot 4} - \frac{f(-2)}{120\times 2\cdot 4} + \frac{f(-1)}{48\times 1\cdot 4}$$

$$- \frac{f(0)}{36\times \cdot 4} + \frac{f(1)}{48\times -\cdot 6} - \frac{f(2)}{120\times -1\cdot 6} + \frac{f(3)}{720\times -2\cdot 6},$$

or $f(\cdot 4) = -\cdot 0046592\, f(-3) + \cdot 0396032\, f(-2) - \cdot 169728\, f(-1)$

$\qquad + \cdot 792064\, f(0) + \cdot 396032\, f(1) - \cdot 0594048\, f(2) + \cdot 0060928\, f(3)$

$\qquad = +\;\; \cdot 05055 - \cdot 00466$

$\qquad\quad\;\; 1\cdot 64665 \quad \cdot 27647$

$\qquad\quad\;\; 1\cdot 05079 \quad \cdot 20117$

$\qquad\qquad\;\; \cdot 02633$

$\qquad \overline{\;\;+2\cdot 77432 - \cdot 48230\;\;}$

$\qquad = \quad\; 2\cdot 29202$ as before.

Note, as a check, that the algebraic sum of the coefficients of the terms on the right-hand side of the above equation is unity.

13. For the sake of completeness it is necessary to refer to a system of notation in connection with central differences which was introduced by W. S. B. Woolhouse and is still in use to some extent. This system of notation is compared with that used in the previous chapters in the following scheme:

Ordinary Notation					*Woolhouse's Notation*			
$f(-2)$					$f(-2)$			
	$\Delta f(-2)$					a_{-2}		
$f(-1)$		$\Delta^2 f(-2)$			$f(-1)$		b_{-1}	
	$\Delta f(-1)$		$\Delta^3 f(-2)$			a_{-1}		c_{-1}
$f(0)$		$\Delta^2 f(-1)$		$\Delta^4 f(-2)$	$f(0)$	(a_0)	b_0	$(c_0)\; d_0$
	$\Delta f(0)$		$\Delta^3 f(-1)$			a_1		c_1
$f(1)$		$\Delta^2 f(0)$			$f(1)$		b_1	
	$\Delta f(1)$					a_2		
$f(2)$					$f(2)$			

where $\Delta f(-2)$, $\Delta^2 f(-2)$, etc. are denoted by a_{-2}, b_{-1}, etc. and

$$a_0 = \tfrac{1}{2}(a_{-1} + a_{+1}),$$
$$c_0 = \tfrac{1}{2}(c_{-1} + c_{+1}).$$

Under this notation Stirling's formula to fourth differences is

$$f(x) = f(0) + x a_0 + \frac{x^2}{2!}\, b_0 + \frac{x(x^2-1)}{3!}\, c_0 + \frac{x^2(x^2-1)}{4!}\, d_0$$

$$= f(0) + \left(a_0 - \frac{c_0}{3!}\right) x + \left(\frac{b_0}{2!} - \frac{d_0}{4!}\right) x^2 + \frac{c_0}{3!}\, x^3 + \frac{d_0}{4!}\, x^4 \quad \dots(11).$$

Similarly Gauss' formula can be written

$$f(x) = f(0) + xa_1 + \frac{x(x-1)}{2!}b_0 + \frac{(x+1)x(x-1)}{3!}c_1$$
$$+ \frac{(x+1)x(x-1)(x-2)}{4!}d_0 \quad \ldots\ldots(12).$$

14. Another system of notation, which is extensively used, is that due to W. F. Sheppard. Two operators δ and μ are used, such that

$$\delta f(-\tfrac{1}{2}) = f(0) - f(-1), \qquad \mu f(\tfrac{1}{2}) = \tfrac{1}{2}[f(0) + f(1)],$$
$$\delta f(\tfrac{1}{2}) = f(1) - f(0), \qquad \mu \delta f(0) = \tfrac{1}{2}[\delta f(\tfrac{1}{2}) + \delta f(-\tfrac{1}{2})],$$
$$\text{etc.} \qquad\qquad\qquad \text{etc.}$$

This notation, although somewhat complicated, gives the usual central difference formulas in very convenient forms.

CHAPTER VI

FINITE DIFFERENCES. INVERSE INTERPOLATION

1. In direct interpolation a series of values of the function is given and the problem is to find the value of the function corresponding to some intermediate value of the argument.

In *Inverse Interpolation* the problem is reversed and it is required to find the value of the argument which corresponds to some value of the function, intermediate between two tabulated values.

2. In certain cases of mathematical functions the desired result can be obtained by direct calculation. Thus if

$$y = f(x) = a^x,$$

$$x = \frac{\log y}{\log a},$$

and the value of x can be found equivalent to any given value of y.

Where this is not the case various methods can be adopted. These will be examined in order.

3. Let $y = f(x)$ be the given value. Then

$$y = f(x) = f(0) + x\Delta f(0) + \frac{x(x-1)}{2!}\Delta^2 f(0) + \ldots.$$

If it be assumed that the higher orders of differences vanish, and that the values of Δ, Δ^2, etc. are obtained from the given terms of the series, then we have an equation in x which can be solved by the usual methods.

The disadvantages of this plan are firstly that an equation of higher degree than the second is troublesome to solve, and secondly that for certain functions the degree of approximation may not be very close. Since a quadratic equation employs only three terms of the series, it often happens that no close approximation can be obtained. In all cases the intervals between terms should be as narrow as possible, so that accuracy may be increased and the use of higher orders of differences obviated as far as possible.

4. This difficulty of solving an equation in x of higher degree than the second can be overcome in two ways. Assume, for purposes of illustration, that four values of the function are given, viz. $f(0)$, $f(1), f(2)$ and $f(3)$.

Then

$$f(x) = f(0) + x\Delta f(0) + \frac{x(x-1)}{2!}\Delta^2 f(0) + \frac{x(x-1)(x-2)}{3!}\Delta^3 f(0).$$

No further differences can be calculated and therefore, since $f(x)$ is known, the corresponding value of x is found by the solution of a cubic equation in x. The solution of the cubic can however be avoided by proceeding as follows:

Taking three terms only at a time

$$f(x) = f(0) + x\Delta f(0) + \frac{x(x-1)}{2!}\Delta^2 f(0),$$

and $\qquad f(x) = f(1) + (x-1)\Delta f(1) + \frac{(x-1)(x-2)}{2!}\Delta^2 f(1).$

The third difference error in the first equation is

$$\frac{x(x-1)(x-2)}{3!}\Delta^3 f(0),$$

and, in the second equation,

$$\frac{(x-1)(x-2)(x-3)}{3!}\Delta^3 f(1).$$

If now both sides of these equations be multiplied respectively by $(3 - x')$ and x' (where x' is a rough approximation to the required value, obtained by inspection) and the equations so weighted be added together, a new quadratic equation in x will be formed from which the third difference error will be practically eliminated. The work of solving a cubic equation has been avoided, but all terms have been used without sensible loss in accuracy.

If the mere arithmetic mean of the equations were taken, without weighting as above, it is possible that, in certain cases, a worse result would be obtained by taking four terms instead of three.

5. Alternatively the solution of the equation may be obtained by successive degrees of approximation.

Thus, taking the above equation and neglecting differences of the second and higher orders, we obtain as a first approximation the value x_1, where

$$x_1 = \frac{f(x) - f(0)}{\Delta f(0)} \quad\ldots\ldots\ldots\ldots\ldots\ldots(1).$$

A further approximation is obtained by taking second differences into account and writing x_1 in place of x in the equation, thus giving

$$x_2 = \frac{f(x) - f(0)}{\Delta f(0) + \frac{1}{2}(x_1 - 1)\,\Delta^2 f(0)} \quad\cdots\cdots\cdots\cdots(2).$$

When third differences are taken into account x_2 is written for x, giving

$$x_3 = \frac{f(x) - f(0)}{\Delta f(0) + \frac{1}{2}(x_2 - 1)\,\Delta^2 f(0) + \frac{1}{6}(x_2 - 1)(x_2 - 2)\,\Delta^3 f(0)} \quad\cdots(3).$$

These processes can be repeated until the desired degree of approximation is reached. The method has the disadvantage of being somewhat laborious. On the other hand it has the advantage that an error of calculation at an early stage does not vitiate the result, being rectified by the further approximations.

6. A different method of procedure is to treat x as a function of $f(x)$. Thus since

$$y = f(x),$$

we may write

$$x = \phi(y).$$

We therefore treat x as a function of y and, since the given values of y (i.e. $f(0)$, $f(1)$, etc.) will usually represent unequal intervals of the variable y, we must resort to interpolation by such a method as Lagrange's or Divided Differences, in order to obtain our value of x (i.e. $\phi(y)$) corresponding to the given value of $f(x)$.

7. The following example is worked out in each of the above ways.

Example. Find the number of which the log is $2\frac{1}{8}$, having given

$$\log 200 = 2\cdot30103$$
$$210 = 2\cdot32222$$
$$220 = 2\cdot34242$$
$$230 = 2\cdot36173.$$

Method I.

$f(x)$	Δ	Δ^2	Δ^3
2·30103	·02119	− ·00099	·00010
2·32222	·02020	− ·00089	
2·34242	·01931		
2·36173			

$$f(x) = 2\cdot33333 = 2\cdot30103 + \cdot02119\,x - \cdot00099\,\frac{x\,(x-1)}{2}$$
$$+ \cdot00010\,\frac{x\,(x-1)\,(x-2)}{6}.$$

Or, by reduction,

$$x^3 - 32\cdot7\,x^2 + 1303\cdot1\,x - 1938 = 0.$$

Whence, solving the cubic,

$$x = 1\cdot5443.$$

Since the initial value of x is 200 and the unit of measurement is 10, the result of the calculation is to give 215·443 as the required value of x.

8. *Method II.*

$$f(x) = 2\cdot30103 + \cdot02119\,x - \cdot00099\,\frac{x\,(x-1)}{2},$$

also, $f(x) = 2\cdot32222 + \cdot02020\,(x-1) - \cdot00089\,\dfrac{(x-1)\,(x-2)}{2}.$

The first approximation to the value of x is $x' = 1\cdot5$, so that $3 - x' = 1\cdot5$. Since the values of $3 - x'$ and x' are approximately equal, we may take for our "weighted" equation the arithmetic mean of the above equations, giving

$$f(x) = 2\cdot33333 = 2\cdot30108 + \cdot02161\,x - \cdot00047\,x^2.$$

Whence, solving the quadratic, $x = 1\cdot5443$ as before.

9. *Method III.*

1st approximation

$$x_1 = \frac{2\cdot33333 - 2\cdot30103}{\cdot02119} = 1\cdot5243,$$

2nd approximation

$$x_2 = \frac{2\cdot33333 - 2\cdot30103}{\cdot02119 - \frac{1}{2} \times \cdot5243 \times \cdot00099} = 1\cdot5432,$$

3rd approximation

$$x_3 = \frac{2\cdot33333 - 2\cdot30103}{\cdot02119 - \frac{1}{2} \times \cdot5432 \times \cdot00099 + \frac{1}{6} \times \cdot5432 \times (\cdot5432 - 1) \times \cdot00010}$$
$$= 1\cdot5442,$$

which differs only slightly from the value obtained by Methods I and II.

10. *Method IV.* Under this method we may consider the data to be as follows:

u	$f(x)$
2·30103	200
2·32222	210
2·34242	220
2·36173	230

It is required to find the value of $f(2\cdot33333)$. By Lagrange,

$$f(2\cdot33333) = \frac{(\cdot01111)(-\cdot00909)(-\cdot02840)}{(-\cdot02119)(-\cdot04139)(-\cdot06070)} \times 200$$

$$+ \frac{(\cdot03230)(-\cdot00909)(-\cdot02840)}{(\cdot02119)(-\cdot02020)(-\cdot03951)} \times 210$$

$$+ \frac{(\cdot03230)(\cdot01111)(-\cdot02840)}{(\cdot04139)(\cdot02020)(-\cdot01931)} \times 220$$

$$+ \frac{(\cdot03230)(\cdot01111)(-\cdot00909)}{(\cdot06070)(\cdot03951)(\cdot01931)} \times 230$$

$$= -10\cdot7748 + 103\cdot5416 + 138\cdot8764 - 16\cdot2006$$

$$= 215\cdot443.$$

This result agrees with the values previously found. The true value is 215·442 and it will be seen, therefore, that all of these methods give results in this case which are closely approximate to the true value.

11. Methods I—III differ from Method IV, in that the first three methods assume that $f(x)$ is a parabolic function of x, whereas Method IV assumes that x can be expressed as a parabolic function of $f(x)$. Both these assumptions may be sufficiently accurate in many cases, but in other cases an inspection of the trend of the given values of the function may indicate which assumption is to be preferred.

12. By the use of the formulas of Divided Differences given in Chapter VIII, Methods I—III can be applied to cases where the given values of the function are at unequal intervals.

The application of Method IV is, of course, perfectly general.

CHAPTER VII

FINITE DIFFERENCES. SUMMATION OR INTEGRATION

1. *Summation* is the process of finding the sum of any number of terms of a given series. This can be accomplished either if the law of the series is known or if a sufficient number of terms is given to enable the law to be ascertained. As will be shown in Chapter XX, if no mathematical law is apparent, methods can be applied by which the approximate sum of a series can be obtained.

2. Consider a function $F(x)$ whose 1st difference is $f(x)$. Then we have

$$F(1) \quad - F(0) \quad = f(0)$$
$$F(2) \quad - F(1) \quad = f(1)$$
$$\vdots \qquad \quad \vdots \qquad \quad \vdots$$
$$F(a) \quad - F(a-1) = f(a-1)$$
$$F(a+1) - F(a) \quad = f(a)$$
$$\vdots \qquad \quad \vdots \qquad \quad \vdots$$
$$F(n-1) - F(n-2) = f(n-2)$$
$$F(n) \quad - F(n-1) = f(n-1).$$

Summing both sides, we obtain

$$F(n) - F(0) = f(0) + f(1) \quad + \ldots + f(n-1)$$

or $\quad F(a) - F(0) = f(0) + f(1) \quad + \ldots + f(a-1)$

or $\quad F(n) - F(a) = f(a) + f(a+1) + \ldots + f(n-1) \quad \ldots(1).$

It is clear, therefore, that the sum of any number of terms of a series of values of $f(x)$ can be represented by the difference between two values of another function $F(x)$ whose 1st difference is $f(x)$. By analogy with the system of notation already adopted for expressing orders of differences, the process of finding the function whose 1st difference is $f(x)$ may be denoted by $\Delta^{-1} f(x)$. It is customary to express $f(0) + f(1) + \ldots + f(n-1)$ as $\sum_{0}^{n-1} f(x)$, the terms at which the summation is commenced and terminated (designated respectively the *inferior* and *superior* limits of summation) being indicated in the manner shown.

3. The process of finding the value of $F(x)$ is known as *Finite Integration* and $F(x)$ is called the *Finite Integral* of $f(x)$. Where the limits of summation are known we obtain by summation of $f(x)$ the *Definite Integral* of $f(x)$; if the limits of summation are not expressed we obtain merely the *Indefinite Integral* of $f(x)$.

4. As stated above, in obtaining the indefinite integral of $f(x)$ no point is specified at which the summation is to commence and, since an unknown number of terms of the series is included, it is necessary to include in the value of $F(x)$ a constant term which is of unknown value.

This constant vanishes in the case of definite integrals, since if

$$\Sigma f(x) = F(x) + c,$$

then
$$\overset{n-1}{\underset{0}{\Sigma}} f(x) = [F(n) + c] - [F(0) + c]$$
$$= F(n) - F(0).$$

5. It is obviously always possible to find the first difference of any function, but it does not follow that every function can be integrated. The functions which can be integrated are limited in number and the process of integration rests largely on the ingenuity of the solver aided by such analogous forms as may be obtained by the formulas of finite differences.

Thus we have $\Delta a^x = (a-1) a^x,$

whence it is easily seen that

$$a^x = \frac{\Delta a^x}{a-1},$$

and therefore, since the result of differencing $\dfrac{a^x}{a-1}$ is to give a^x, we have

$$\Sigma a^x = \frac{a^x}{a-1} + c,$$

where c is the constant introduced by integration.

The sum of the series $a^r + a^{r+1} + \ldots + a^{r+n-1}$ is at once obtained by finding the value of the definite integral $\overset{r+n-1}{\underset{r}{\Sigma}} a^x$, which by § 2 is equal to $\dfrac{a^{r+n}}{a-1} - \dfrac{a^r}{a-1}$, which agrees with the familiar result for the sum of a geometrical progression.

6. Similarly since $\quad \Delta x^{(m)} = m x^{(m-1)},$

by analogy $\quad\quad\quad \Sigma x^{(m)} = \dfrac{x^{(m+1)}}{m+1} + c.$

7. The following table gives the values of some of the simpler integrals. They should be verified as an exercise by the student.

Function	Indefinite Integral
x	$\dfrac{x(x-1)}{2} + c$
a^x	$\dfrac{a^x}{a-1} + c$
$x^{(m)}$	$\dfrac{x^{(m+1)}}{m+1} + c$
$x^{(-m)}$	$\dfrac{x^{(-m-1)}}{-(m-1)} + c$
$(ax+b)(a\overline{x-1}+b)\ldots(a\overline{x-m+1}+b)$	$\dfrac{(ax+b)(a\overline{x-1}+b)\ldots(a\overline{x-m}+b)}{a(m+1)} + c$
$(ax+b)(a\overline{x+1}+b)\ldots(a\overline{x+m-1}+b)$	$\dfrac{(a\overline{x-1}+b)(ax+b)\ldots(a\overline{x+m-1}+b)}{a(m+1)} + c$
$\dfrac{1}{(ax+b)(a\overline{x+1}+b)\ldots(a\overline{x+m-1}+b)}$	$\dfrac{1}{-a(m-1)(ax+b)(a\overline{x+1}+b)\ldots(a\overline{x+m-2}+b)} + c$
$\dfrac{1}{(ax+b)(a\overline{x-1}+b)\ldots(a\overline{x-m+1}+b)}$	$\dfrac{1}{-a(m-1)(a\overline{x-1}+b)\ldots(a\overline{x-m+1}+b)} + c$

8. If the form of the function is unknown, a general formula for the sum of a series of values may be obtained as follows, since

$$f(x) = f(0) + x\Delta f(0) + \frac{x(x-1)}{2!}\Delta^2 f(0)$$
$$+ \frac{x(x-1)(x-2)}{3!}\Delta^3 f(0) + \ldots$$

Integrating both sides, we have

$$\Sigma f(x) = c + xf(0) + \frac{x(x-1)}{2!}\Delta f(0) + \frac{x(x-1)(x-2)}{3!}\Delta^2 f(0) + \ldots,$$

or, integrating between limits, we have

$$\sum_{0}^{n-1} f(x) = nf(0) + \frac{n(n-1)}{2!}\Delta f(0) + \frac{n(n-1)(n-2)}{3!}\Delta^2 f(0) + \ldots$$

or, more generally,

$$\overset{a+n-1}{\underset{a}{\Sigma}} f(x) = f(a) + f(a+1) + \dots + f(a+n-1)$$

$$= nf(a) + \frac{n(n-1)}{2!} \Delta f(a) + \frac{n(n-1)(n-2)}{3!} \Delta^2 f(a) + \dots$$

$$\dots\dots\dots(2).$$

It is instructive to obtain this result by the method of separation of symbols. For

$$f(a) = f(a),$$
$$f(a+1) = (1+\Delta)f(a),$$
$$f(a+2) = (1+\Delta)^2 f(a),$$
$$\vdots \qquad \vdots$$
$$f(a+n-1) = (1+\Delta)^{n-1} f(a).$$

Adding

$$\overset{a+n-1}{\underset{a}{\Sigma}} f(a) = \{1 + (1+\Delta) + (1+\Delta)^2 + \dots + (1+\Delta)^{n-1}\} f(a)$$

$$= \frac{(1+\Delta)^n - 1}{(1+\Delta) - 1} f(a)$$

$$= \frac{\left\{1 + n\Delta + \frac{n(n-1)}{2!}\Delta^2 + \dots - 1\right\}}{\Delta} f(a)$$

$$= \left\{n + \frac{n(n-1)}{2!}\Delta + \frac{n(n-1)(n-2)}{3!}\Delta^2 + \dots\right\} f(a)$$

$$= nf(a) + \frac{n(n-1)}{2!}\Delta f(a) + \frac{n(n-1)(n-2)}{3!}\Delta^2 f(a) + \dots.$$

9. An example will illustrate the use of the formula.

Example 1. Find the sum of the first n terms of the series whose initial terms are 1, 8, 27, 64, 125.

We have

$f(x)$	Δ	Δ^2	Δ^3	Δ^4
1	7	12	6	0
8	19	18	6	
27	37	24		
64	61			
125				

Whence

$$\sum_{0}^{n-1} f(x) = n \times 1 + \frac{n(n-1)}{2!} \times 7 + \frac{n(n-1)(n-2)}{3!} \times 12$$

$$+ \frac{n(n-1)(n-2)(n-3)}{4!} \times 6$$

$$= \frac{n(n^3 + 2n^2 + n)}{4} = \frac{n^2(n+1)^2}{4},$$

which agrees with the formula for the sum of the cubes of the natural numbers.

10. Where it is desired to integrate a function which is the product of two factors, the following device may often be utilised with advantage.

Let the function be $\qquad y = u_x v_x.$

Then $\qquad \Delta u_x v_x = u_{x+1} v_{x+1} - u_x v_x$

$$= u_{x+1}(v_{x+1} - v_x) + v_x(u_{x+1} - u_x)$$

$$= u_{x+1} \Delta v_x + v_x \Delta u_x.$$

Integrating both sides of the equation, we obtain

$$u_x v_x = \Sigma u_{x+1} \Delta v_x + \Sigma v_x \Delta u_x$$

or $\qquad \Sigma v_x \Delta u_x = u_x v_x - \Sigma u_{x+1} \Delta v_x \quad \dots\dots\dots\dots\dots\dots(3).$

Thus, if the original function can be put in the form $v_x \Delta u_x$, its integral can be made to depend upon that of $u_{x+1} \Delta v_x$, and, if the latter is in a form which can be readily integrated, the value of an apparently intractable integral may often be obtained in this way.

Example 2. To find the value of $\Sigma x a^x$.

Since $\Sigma a^x = \dfrac{a^x}{a-1}$, we may write

$$\Sigma x a^x = \Sigma x \frac{\Delta a^x}{a-1}.$$

Using the above formula (3) we get

$$\Sigma x \frac{\Delta a^x}{a-1} = \frac{x a^x}{a-1} - \Sigma \frac{a^{x+1}}{a-1} \Delta x$$

$$= \frac{x a^x}{a-1} - \Sigma \frac{a^{x+1}}{a-1}, \text{ since } \Delta x = 1,$$

$$= \frac{x a^x}{a-1} - \frac{a^{x+1}}{(a-1)^2} + c.$$

11. Sometimes it may be necessary to apply the formula more than once in order to reduce the integral by stages to a standard form. The process is illustrated in the following example.

Example 3. To find the value of $\Sigma 2^x x^3$.

Remembering that $\Delta 2^x = 2^x$, we may write

$$\Sigma 2^x x^3 = \Sigma x^3 \Delta 2^x$$
$$= x^3 2^x - \Sigma 2^{x+1} \Delta x^3$$
$$= x^3 2^x - \Sigma 2^{x+1} (3x^2 + 3x + 1).$$

It will be observed that in applying formula (3), the degree of x, in the terms within the integral, has been reduced by unity. Proceeding as before we obtain

$$\Sigma 2^x x^3 = x^3 2^x - \Sigma (3x^2 + 3x + 1) \Delta 2^{x+1}$$
$$= x^3 2^x - [2^{x+1}(3x^2 + 3x + 1) - \Sigma 2^{x+2} \Delta (3x^2 + 3x + 1)]$$
$$= 2^x (x^3 - 6x^2 - 6x - 2) + \Sigma 2^{x+2} (6x + 6)$$
$$= 2^x (x^3 - 6x^2 - 6x - 2) + \Sigma (6x + 6) \Delta 2^{x+2}$$
$$= 2^x (x^3 - 6x^2 - 6x - 2) + [2^{x+2}(6x + 6) - \Sigma 2^{x+3} \Delta (6x + 6)]$$
$$= 2^x (x^3 - 6x^2 + 18x + 22) - \Sigma 2^{x+3} \times 6$$
$$= 2^x (x^3 - 6x^2 + 18x + 22) - 6 \times 2^{x+3} + c$$
$$= 2^x (x^3 - 6x^2 + 18x - 26) + c.$$

The above process is analogous to that of "Integration by Parts," which is dealt with in the Integral Calculus, Chapter XVIII, § 6.

CHAPTER VIII

FINITE DIFFERENCES. DIVIDED DIFFERENCES

1. A simple method of interpolation is available, where the intervals between the given terms are unequal, by the method of *Divided Differences*.

2. The application of the method rests upon the assumption, which, as has been shown, is the basis of all theorems for interpolation by means of Finite Differences, that $f(x)$ is a rational integral function of x of the nth degree.

On this assumption, it can be shown that $f(x)$ can be expressed in the form

$$A_0 + A_1(x - a_1) + A_2(x - a_1)(x - a_2) + \ldots$$
$$+ A_n(x - a_1)(x - a_2) \ldots (x - a_n),$$

where $A_0, A_1, \ldots A_n, a_1, a_2, \ldots a_n$ are constants.

3. In order to apply this formula in practice, it is convenient to introduce a scheme of notation on the following lines, where the symbol of operation is denoted by Δ' in order to distinguish it from the ordinary Δ.

Value of x	Value of Function	Δ'	Δ'^2	Δ'^3	etc.
0	$f(0)$	$\dfrac{f(a_1) - f(0)}{a_1}$	$\dfrac{\Delta' f(a_1) - \Delta' f(0)}{a_2}$	$\dfrac{\Delta'^2 f(a_1) - \Delta'^2 f(0)}{a_3}$	
a_1	$f(a_1)$	$\dfrac{f(a_2) - f(a_1)}{a_2 - a_1}$	$\dfrac{\Delta' f(a_2) - \Delta' f(a_1)}{a_3 - a_1}$	$\dfrac{\Delta'^2 f(a_2) - \Delta'^2 f(a_1)}{a_4 - a_1}$	
a_2	$f(a_2)$	$\dfrac{f(a_3) - f(a_2)}{a_3 - a_2}$	$\dfrac{\Delta' f(a_3) - \Delta' f(a_2)}{a_4 - a_2}$	$\vdots$	
a_3	$f(a_3)$	$\dfrac{f(a_4) - f(a_3)}{a_4 - a_3}$	$\vdots$		
a_4	$f(a_4)$	$\vdots$			
$\vdots$	$\vdots$				

Generally, we have

$$\Delta'^n f(a_r) = \frac{\Delta'^{n-1} f(a_{r+1}) - \Delta'^{n-1} f(a_r)}{a_{n+r} - a_r}.$$

Hence $\quad f(a_1) = f(0) + a_1 \Delta' f(0),$

and $\qquad f(a_2) = f(a_1) + (a_2 - a_1) \Delta' f(a_1)$

$$= f(0) + a_1 \Delta' f(0) + (a_2 - a_1)\{\Delta' f(0) + a_2 \Delta'^2 f(0)\}$$

$$= f(0) + a_2 \Delta' f(0) + a_2 (a_2 - a_1) \Delta'^2 f(0).$$

By proceeding similarly for further terms, we find that we can write generally

$$f(x) = f(0) + x \Delta' f(0) + x(x - a_1) \Delta'^2 f(0)$$
$$+ x(x - a_1)(x - a_2) \Delta'^3 f(0) + \dots \quad (1).$$

This general form can be readily established by the method of induction.

By giving appropriate values to $a_1, a_2, \dots$ the ordinary formulas applicable to equal intervals can be at once deduced.

4. The general method of working will be shown more simply by an example.

Example. Find the value of log 4·0180, having given the following data:

Number	Logarithm
4·0000	·6020600
4·0127	·6034367
4·0233	·6045824
4·0298	·6052835
4·0369	·6060480

Transposing the origin, we have the following scheme:

x	$f(x)$	Δ'	Δ'^2
0·0000	·6020600	$\dfrac{·0013767}{·0127} = ·108402$	$\dfrac{-·000317}{·0233} = -·0136$
0·0127	·6034367	$\dfrac{·0011457}{·0106} = ·108085$	$\dfrac{-·000223}{·0171} = -·0130$
0·0233	·6045824	$\dfrac{·0007011}{·0065} = ·107862$	$\dfrac{-·000186}{·0136} = -·0137$
0·0298	·6052835	$\dfrac{·0007645}{·0071} = ·107676$	
0·0369	·6060480		

We have to find $f(\cdot 0180)$, which is, by the above formula,

$$f(0) + \cdot 0180 \Delta' f(0) + \cdot 0180 \times \cdot 0053 \Delta'^2 f(0)$$

[the further terms will not affect the seventh place of decimals],

where $f(0) = \cdot 6020600$, $\Delta' f(0) = \cdot 108402$, $\Delta'^2 f(0) = - \cdot 0136$.

Thus $\log 4 \cdot 0180 = \cdot 6020600 + \cdot 00195124 - \cdot 00000130 = \cdot 6040099$ to seven decimal places, which agrees exactly with the true result.

CHAPTER IX

FINITE DIFFERENCES. FUNCTIONS OF TWO VARIABLES

1. Questions involving functions of two variables arise frequently in actuarial practice. Thus the tabulated values of functions (e.g. annuities) dependent upon two lives may be given only for combinations of quinquennial ages in order to economise space. If the value corresponding to any other combination of ages is required, resort must be had to methods of interpolation.

2. In considering the problem of the changes induced in the value of $f(x, y)$ by finite changes in the values of x and y we must consider x and y as being independent of each other. Clearly, if y were a function of x the expression $f(x, y)$ could be made to assume the form of a function of x alone and it could be dealt with by the methods already developed in previous chapters.

Thus x may vary while y remains constant, so that, if x changes to $x + h$, the value of the function becomes $f(x + h, y)$; or y can vary while x remains constant, giving a value $f(x, y + k)$; or both x and y can vary independently, giving a value for the function of $f(x + h, y + k)$.

3. We shall proceed first to discuss the problem where the values of the function are given for combinations of successive equidistant values of x and y.

Thus we may have

$$f(x, y) \qquad f(x + h, y) \qquad f(x + 2h, y) \qquad \ldots f(x + mh, y)$$
$$f(x, y + k) \quad f(x + h, y + k) \quad f(x + 2h, y + k) \quad \ldots f(x + mh, y + k)$$
$$\vdots \qquad\qquad \vdots \qquad\qquad \vdots \qquad\qquad\qquad \vdots$$
$$f(x, y + nk) \quad f(x + h, y + nk) \quad f(x + 2h, y + nk) \quad \ldots f(x + mh, y + nk)$$

As has already been seen in the case of functions of one variable (Chapter III, § 6), this scheme can be simplified, for the origin can be placed at the point (x, y), and the unit of measurement can be taken as h in the case of the variable x and k in the case of the variable y.

The scheme then becomes

$f(0, 0)$ $f(1, 0)$ $f(2, 0)$..............$f(m, 0)$

$f(0, 1)$ $f(1, 1)$ $f(2, 1)$..............$f(m, 1)$

$\vdots$ $\vdots$ $\vdots$ $\vdots$

$f(0, n)$ $f(1, n)$ $f(2, n)$ ....$f(m, n)$

4. Since x and y may vary independently, a fresh scheme of notation must be introduced to express the variations which may arise. Thus Δ_x will be used to denote the operation of differencing with respect to x, y remaining constant, a corresponding significance attaching to Δ_y, so that

$$\Delta_x f(0, 0) = f(1, 0) - f(0, 0),$$

$$\Delta_y f(0, 0) = f(0, 1) - f(0, 0),$$

or, using the method of separation of symbols,

$$f(1, 0) = (1 + \Delta_x)f(0, 0).$$

Accordingly, we have

$$f(m, n) = (1 + \Delta_x)^m (1 + \Delta_y)^n f(0, 0)$$

$$= \left(1 + m\Delta_x + \binom{m}{2}\Delta^2_x + \ldots\right)\left(1 + n\Delta_y + \binom{n}{2}\Delta^2_y + \ldots\right)f(0, 0)$$

$$= f(0, 0) + m\Delta_x f(0,0) + \binom{m}{2}\Delta^2_x f(0, 0) + \binom{m}{3}\Delta^3_x f(0, 0) + \ldots$$

$$+ n\Delta_y f(0,0) + mn\,\Delta_x\Delta_y f(0,0) + \binom{m}{2}n\Delta^2_x\Delta_y f(0, 0) + \ldots$$

$$+ \binom{n}{2}\Delta^2_y f(0, 0) + m\binom{n}{2}\Delta_x\Delta^2_y f(0,0) + \ldots$$

$$+ \binom{n}{3}\Delta^3_y f(0, 0) + \ldots$$

$$\ldots\ldots\ldots(1).$$

Here Δ^2_x, Δ^3_x, ... can be written down by differencing the *rows* of the table of the function; similarly Δ^2_y, Δ^3_y, ... are the differences of the *columns* of the table.

To find $\Delta_x \Delta_y$, $\Delta^2_x \Delta_y$, etc. we have

$$\Delta_x \Delta_y f(0, 0) = \Delta_x [f(0, 1) - f(0, 0)]$$
$$= f(1, 1) - f(0, 1) - f(1, 0) + f(0, 0),$$
$$\Delta^2_x \Delta_y f(0, 0) = \Delta^2_x [f(0, 1) - f(0, 0)]$$
$$= f(2, 1) - 2f(1, 1) + f(0, 1) - f(2, 0)$$
$$+ 2f(1, 0) - f(0, 0),$$

and so on.

Example 1. Table XVI of the "Short Collection of Actuarial Tables." To find $A_{31:63}^{1}$, having given

$$A_{30:60}^{1} = \cdot 11669, \qquad A_{35:60}^{1} = \cdot 13190, \qquad A_{40:60}^{1} = \cdot 15494,$$
$$A_{30:65}^{1} = \cdot 09809, \qquad A_{35:65}^{1} = \cdot 11039,$$
$$A_{30:70}^{1} = \cdot 07812.$$

Here $m = \frac{1}{5}$, $n = \frac{3}{5}$, and

$$\Delta_x = \quad \cdot 01521, \qquad \Delta^2_x = \quad \cdot 00783, \qquad \Delta_x \Delta_y = - \cdot 00291,$$
$$\Delta_y = - \cdot 01860, \qquad \Delta^2_y = - \cdot 00137.$$

Whence $A_{31:63}^{1} = \cdot 10776$, the correct value being $\cdot 10773$.

5. An obvious method of procedure involving only first differences is as follows. Obtain the value of $f(0, n)$ by interpolation between the values of $f(0, 0)$ and $f(0, 1)$. Similarly, obtain the value of $f(1, n)$ from the values of $f(1, 0)$ and $f(1, 1)$. Finally find $f(m, n)$ by interpolation between $f(0, n)$ and $f(1, n)$. Thus

$$f(0, \ n) = \overline{1 - n} f(0, 0) + n f(0, 1),$$
$$f(1, \ n) = \overline{1 - n} f(1, 0) + n f(1, 1),$$
$$f(m, n) = \overline{1 - m} f(0, n) + m f(1, n)$$
$$= f(0, 0) + m \Delta_x f(0, 0) + n \Delta_y f(0, 0) + mn \Delta_x \Delta_y f(0, 0)$$
$$\cdots \cdots \cdots (2)$$
$$= \overline{1 - m} \; \overline{1 - n} f(0, 0) + n . \overline{1 - m} f(0, 1)$$
$$+ m . \overline{1 - n} f(1, 0) + mn f(1, 1) \dots (3).$$

Employing this formula in the example given above we find

$$A_{31:63}^{1} = \cdot 10822.$$

The method is suitable if only a rough approximation is required, but cannot be depended upon to give an accurate value.

6. Obviously the method can be extended by taking higher orders of differences. The disadvantage of this procedure is that it involves the calculation of further values of the function corresponding to a given value of x as a preliminary to applying the interpolation formula to find the value of $f(x, y)$. The process thus becomes laborious and moreover we do not necessarily obtain identical values for $f(x, y)$ if we interpolate first with regard to x and then with regard to y, or *vice versa*.

7. As in the case of functions of one variable, we shall expect to obtain the best results when the principles of central differences are applied, i.e. when the required term occupies as nearly as possible a central position among the terms employed in the formula. The difficulty is that, in dealing with functions of two variables, we cannot adapt our formulas to any system of values which may be given. Thus an inspection of the advancing difference formula (1) shows that it involves points whose coordinates form a triangular plan which may be illustrated thus:

$$\vdots$$

$(0, 2)$
o

$(0, 1)$ $(1, 1)$
o   o

$(0, 0)$ $(1, 0)$ $(2, 0)$
o   o   o

This illustrates the formula where two orders of differences are taken into account, the black dot representing the interpolated term. It will be seen that the scheme is hardly satisfactory from the point of view of central differences. For most practical purposes, however, where ordinary actuarial functions are involved, formula (1) will give satisfactory results.

8. Formulas embodying the principles of central differences can conveniently be obtained by an adaptation of Lagrange's formula. This formula applied to functions of two variables has not the same wide application as the ordinary formula of Lagrange previously given in Chapter IV, but, as will be seen below, it gives expressions for $f(x, y)$ in terms of the neighbouring values.

9. *General formula for 4 points.*

Taking all combinations of two terms except those which give rise to x^2 and y^2, let

$$f(x, y) = A\,(x - \beta)\,(y - b) + B\,(x - \beta)\,(y - a) + C\,(x - a)\,(y - a)$$
$$+ D\,(x - a)\,(y - b),$$

then
$$f(a, a) = A\,(a - \beta)\,(a - b),$$
$$f(a, b) = B\,(a - \beta)\,(b - a),$$
$$f(\beta, a) = D\,(\beta - a)\,(a - b),$$
$$f(\beta, b) = C\,(\beta - a)\,(b - a),$$

whence, substituting for A, B, C and D in the original formula,

$$f(x, y) = f(a, a)\frac{(x - \beta)(y - b)}{(a - \beta)(a - b)} + f(a, b)\frac{(x - \beta)(y - a)}{(a - \beta)(b - a)}$$
$$+ f(\beta, b)\frac{(x - a)(y - a)}{(\beta - a)(b - a)} + f(\beta, a)\frac{(x - a)(y - b)}{(\beta - a)(a - b)} \dots (4).$$

10. *General formula for 6 points.*

Taking all combinations of two terms, let

$$f(x, y) = A\,(x - \beta)(\,y - b) + B\,(x - \beta)\,(y - a) + C\,(x - a)\,(y - a)$$
$$+ D\,(x - a)(y - b) + E\,(x - a)\,(x - \beta) + F\,(y - a)\,(y - b).$$

Taking the points $a:a$, $a:b$, $a:c$, $\beta:a$, $\beta:b$ and $\gamma:a$, and proceeding as before, we arrive at the result

$$f(x, y) = f(a, a)\left\{\frac{(x - \beta)(y - b)}{(\beta - a)(b - a)} + \frac{(x - a)(x - \beta)}{(\beta - a)(\gamma - a)} + \frac{(y - a)(y - b)}{(b - a)(c - a)}\right\}$$

$$- f(a, b)\left\{\frac{(x - \beta)(y - a)}{(\beta - a)(b - a)} + \frac{(y - a)(y - b)}{(b - a)(c - b)}\right\}$$

$$+ f(a, c)\frac{(y - a)(y - b)}{(c - a)(c - b)}$$

$$- f(\beta, a)\left\{\frac{(x - a)(y - b)}{(\beta - a)(b - a)} + \frac{(x - a)(x - \beta)}{(\beta - a)(\gamma - \beta)}\right\}$$

$$+ f(\beta, b)\frac{(x - a)(y - a)}{(\beta - a)(b - a)}$$

$$+ f(\gamma, a)\frac{(x - a)(x - \beta)}{(\gamma - a)(\gamma - \beta)} \quad\dots\dots\dots\dots\dots\dots(5).$$

11. *General formula for 9 points.*

Taking all combinations of two terms, each involving x, with two terms each involving y, let

$$f(x, y) = A\,(x - \beta)(x - \gamma)(y - b)(y - c)$$
$$+ B(x - \beta)(x - \gamma)(y - a)(y - c) + C(x - \beta)(x - \gamma)(y - a)(y - b)$$
$$+ D(x - a)(x - \gamma)(y - b)(y - c) + E(x - a)(x - \gamma)(y - a)(y - c)$$
$$+ F(x - a)(x - \gamma)(y - a)(y - b) + G(x - a)(x - \beta)(y - b)(y - c)$$
$$+ H(x - a)(x - \beta)(y - a)(y - c) + I(x - a)(x - \beta)(y - a)(y - b).$$

Whence, proceeding as before, we have

$$f(x, y) = f(a, a)\frac{(x - \beta)(x - \gamma)(y - b)(y - c)}{(a - \beta)(a - \gamma)(a - b)(a - c)}$$

$$+ f(a, b)\frac{(x - \beta)(x - \gamma)(y - a)(y - c)}{(a - \beta)(a - \gamma)(b - a)(b - c)}$$

$$+ f(a, c)\frac{(x - \beta)(x - \gamma)(y - a)(y - b)}{(a - \beta)(a - \gamma)(c - a)(c - b)}$$

$$+ f(\beta, a)\frac{(x - a)(x - \gamma)(y - b)(y - c)}{(\beta - a)(\beta - \gamma)(a - b)(a - c)}$$

$$+ f(\beta, b)\frac{(x - a)(x - \gamma)(y - a)(y - c)}{(\beta - a)(\beta - \gamma)(b - a)(b - c)}$$

$$+ f(\beta, c)\frac{(x - a)(x - \gamma)(y - a)(y - b)}{(\beta - a)(\beta - \gamma)(c - a)(c - b)}$$

$$+ f(\gamma, a)\frac{(x - a)(x - \beta)(y - b)(y - c)}{(\gamma - a)(\gamma - \beta)(a - b)(a - c)}$$

$$+ f(\gamma, b)\frac{(x - a)(x - \beta)(y - a)(y - c)}{(\gamma - a)(\gamma - \beta)(b - a)(b - c)}$$

$$+ f(\gamma, c)\frac{(x - a)(x - \beta)(y - a)(y - b)}{(\gamma - a)(\gamma - \beta)(c - a)(c - b)} \quad \ldots\ldots\ldots\ldots(6).$$

12. Formula (4) is the general formula corresponding to the method of § 5; by altering the notation the identity of the two formulas (3) and (4) is apparent.

Formula (5) includes six values of the function, the co-ordinates being related in the manner shown. It will be seen that the formula can be applied to any of the following groups of values, the black dot representing the interpolated value:

(0, 2)
o

               (0, 1) (1, 1)
                o   o

                             (0, 1)
                             o

(0, 1) (1, 1)   (−1, 0) (0, 0)• (1, 0)   (−1, 0) (0, 0) (1, 0)
  o   o   o   o   o   o   o   o

•
(0, 0) (1, 0) (2, 0)   (0, −1)   (−1, −1)• (0, −1)
  o   o   o   o   o   o

       (i)   (ii)   (iii)

               (0, 1) (1, 1)   (1, 1)
                o   o   o

        (−1, 0) (0, 0)• (1, 0)   (−1, 0) (0, 0) (1, 0)
          o   o   o   o   o   o

                  (1, −1)   (−1, −1)   •(1, −1)
                    o   o   o

             (iv)   (v)

Other systems could be written down, but the above are sufficient for purposes of illustration.

System (i) is obviously the same as the advancing difference formula. It is obtained by writing $\alpha = 0$, $\beta = 1$, $\gamma = 2$, $a = 0$, $b = 1$, $c = 2$ in formula (5).

Example 2. Find $A_{31:63}^{1}$ from the data of Example 1, using the Lagrange formula applicable to system (i). It will be found that the same result is obtained.

System (ii) should be expected to give a formula which will be more accurate than the advancing difference formula, since the interpolated term will occupy a more central position in relation to the terms employed. The formula is obtained by putting $\alpha = 0$, $\beta = 1$, $\gamma = -1$, $a = 0$, $b = 1$, $c = -1$ in formula (5). Working on the same example as before and taking the origin at the point (30, 60), the values of the function entering into the formula are

$$A_{25:60}^{1} = \cdot10080, \qquad A_{30:65}^{1} = \cdot09809, \qquad A_{30:60}^{1} = \cdot11669,$$

$$A_{30:55}^{1} = \cdot14006, \qquad A_{35:65}^{1} = \cdot11039, \qquad A_{35:60}^{1} = \cdot13190.$$

We obtain as a result $A_{31:63}^{1} = \cdot10770$. The degree of approximation, though close, has not, in this instance, been improved.

System (iii) is an inversion of system (ii) and should be useful for interpolation where x and y have negative values.

The lack of symmetry of systems (iv) and (v) suggests that they are not likely to yield good results in practice.

13. When nine points are used, as in formula (6), the system is represented by the following diagram:

$$(-1, 1) \quad (0, 1) \quad (1, 1)$$

$$(-1, 0) \quad (0, 0)\bullet \quad (1, 0)$$

$$(-1, -1) \quad (0, -1) \quad (1, -1)$$

It will be seen that this scheme embodies all the principles of central differences and should therefore give good results.

Taking the previous example with the origin at the point $(30, 60)$ the six values entering into the formula for system (ii) are used together with the following additional values:

$$A^1_{25 : 55} = \cdot 08435, \qquad A^1_{25 : 55} = \cdot 12132, \qquad A^1_{35 : 55} = \cdot 15972.$$

Making use of formula (6) the interpolated value is found to be $\cdot 10771$, a slightly better approximation to the true value than those obtained previously.

On general reasoning we should expect a somewhat better result by taking the origin at the point $(30, 65)$ so that the interpolated value would occupy a more central position. The values $A^1_{25 : 55}$, $A^1_{30 : 55}$, $A^1_{35 : 55}$ entering into the immediately preceding calculation are excluded, and the following values introduced:

$$A^1_{25 : 70} = \cdot 06642, \qquad A^1_{30 : 70} = \cdot 07812, \qquad A^1_{35 : 70} = \cdot 08756.$$

On working out the result, however, we arrive at the value $\cdot 10848$, which is a worse approximation than the value obtained by the rough method of § 5.

14. This apparent inconsistency illustrates one of the chief difficulties of interpolating between functions of two variables, namely, that one does not necessarily obtain a better degree of approximation by proceeding to a higher order of differences or by employing more terms in a formula. Changes in the value of $f(x, y)$ occasioned by alterations in the values of x and y may be so considerable that distant terms may have such a disturbing effect upon the formula used as to upset the agreement between the approximate interpolation surface and the true surface which represents $f(x, y)$.

It is thus difficult to say what will be the degree of approximation of a given formula, but an inspection of the course of the differences will be some guide as to the advisability of introducing further terms into the calculation.

15. Other devices may sometimes be adopted which enable the interpolation to be reduced to the work of a single variable interpolation.

Thus, if the sum of x and y is a multiple of 5, by suitably selecting the origin we may write

$$f(x, -x) = f(0, 0) + x\left[f(1, -1) - f(0, 0)\right]$$

$$+ \binom{x}{2}\left[f(2, -2) - 2f(1, -1) + f(0, 0)\right]$$

$$= \frac{\overline{x-1}\,\overline{x-2}}{2}f(0, 0) - x\,.\,\overline{x-2}f(1, -1)$$

$$+ \frac{x\,.\,\overline{x-1}}{2}f(2, -2) \quad \ldots\ldots(7).$$

By referring to the point diagrams on previous pages it will be seen that the process is equivalent to interpolating along a diagonal line running through the various points. The formula is of the advancing difference type; the corresponding central difference formula would preferably be employed in practice.

J. Spencer has given (*J.I.A.* Vol. 40, pp. 296–301) examples of the use of several ingenious methods of this character.

CHAPTER X

DIFFERENTIAL CALCULUS. ELEMENTARY CONCEPTIONS AND DEFINITIONS

1. In the subject of Finite Differences we were concerned with the changes in the value of a function consequent upon finite changes in the value of the independent variable. In the Differential Calculus we consider the relation of Δy to Δx when the value of Δx is made indefinitely small.

The application of the Differential Calculus is largely limited to such values of a function as are finite and continuous, and, unless otherwise stated, this limitation is to be implied in the following demonstrations. In practice these conditions are almost universally fulfilled by functions entering into actuarial calculations.

2. Let $y = f(x)$ and let x receive an increment h. Then the change in the value of y is measured by $f(x+h) - f(x)$ and the *rate of change* of y is $\dfrac{f(x+h) - f(x)}{h}$. The limit of this expression when $h \to 0$ is called the *Differential Coefficient* or *First Derived Function* of $f(x)$ with respect to x.

The operation of obtaining this limit is called *differentiating $f(x)$*.

Using the notation of Finite Differences the differential coefficient becomes

$$\operatorname*{Lt}_{\Delta x \to 0} \frac{\Delta y}{\Delta x}$$

and is variously denoted by $\dfrac{dy}{dx}$, $f'(x)$, $\dot{f}(x)$, $\dfrac{df(x)}{dx}$, $Df(x)$.

The symbol $\dfrac{dy}{dx}$ or its equivalent represents an *operation* of the character described; the elements dy and dx must not be regarded as separate small quantities.

3. The geometrical representation of the differential coefficient is illustrated in the accompanying diagram.

Let the curve shown represent the

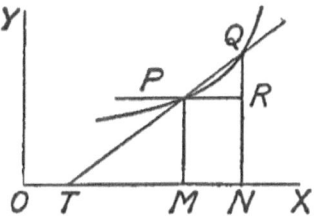

equation $y = f(x)$. Let $OM = x$ and $ON = x + h$, and let PM and QN be the corresponding ordinates. Let PR be the perpendicular from P on QN and let QP be produced to cut OX at T.

Then $\qquad \dfrac{f(x+h) - f(x)}{h} = \dfrac{QN - PM}{MN} = \dfrac{QR}{PR} = \dfrac{PM}{TM} = \tan PTM.$

When the point Q moves up to, and ultimately coincides with the point P, the line QPT becomes the tangent to the curve at the point P. The limiting value of $\dfrac{f(x+h) - f(x)}{h}$ is therefore the tangent of the angle which the tangent to the curve at the point (x, y) makes with the axis of x.

CHAPTER XI

DIFFERENTIAL CALCULUS. STANDARD FORMS. PARTIAL DIFFERENTIATION

1. The differential coefficient of any particular function can, of course, be obtained by direct calculation, but the process can usually be simplified by the application of the following general rules. The general similarity to the propositions already demonstrated for Finite Differences will be apparent.

I. *The differential coefficient of any constant term is zero.*

This is evident since a constant is a quantity which does not change in value in any mathematical operation.

II. *The differential coefficient of the product of a constant and a function of x is equal to the product of the constant and of the differential coefficient of the function.*

Thus
$$\frac{d}{dx}[c \cdot f(x)] = \underset{h \to 0}{\text{Lt}} \frac{cf(x+h) - cf(x)}{h}$$

$$= \underset{h \to 0}{\text{Lt}} \, c\frac{f(x+h) - f(x)}{h}$$

$$= c\frac{df(x)}{dx} \quad \dots\dots\dots\dots\dots\dots(1).$$

III. *The differential coefficient of the algebraic sum of a number of functions of x is the sum of the differential coefficients of the several functions.*

Let $y = u + v + w + \dots$, where $u, v, w, \dots$ are functions of x,

then
$$\Delta y = \Delta u + \Delta v + \Delta w + \dots$$

and
$$\frac{\Delta y}{\Delta x} = \frac{\Delta u}{\Delta x} + \frac{\Delta v}{\Delta x} + \frac{\Delta w}{\Delta x} + \dots,$$

which, by proceeding to the limit, becomes
$$\frac{dy}{dx} = \frac{du}{dx} + \frac{dv}{dx} + \frac{dw}{dx} + \dots \quad \dots\dots\dots\dots(2).$$

IV. *The differential coefficient of the product of two functions is the sum of the products of each function and the differential coefficient of the other.*

Let
$$y = uv,$$
where u and v are both functions of x.

Then
$$\Delta y = (u + \Delta u)(v + \Delta v) - uv$$
$$= u\Delta v + v\Delta u + \Delta u \Delta v$$
$$= u\Delta v + (v + \Delta v)\Delta u$$

and
$$\frac{\Delta y}{\Delta x} = u\frac{\Delta v}{\Delta x} + (v + \Delta v)\frac{\Delta u}{\Delta x},$$

whence, taking the limit, when $v + \Delta v \rightarrow v$,
$$\frac{dy}{dx} = u\frac{dv}{dx} + v\frac{du}{dx} \quad\dots\dots\dots\dots\dots\dots(3),$$

which may be written
$$\frac{1}{y}\frac{dy}{dx} = \frac{1}{u}\frac{du}{dx} + \frac{1}{v}\frac{dv}{dx} \quad\dots\dots\dots\dots\dots(4).$$

This result may be extended to include the product of any number of functions.

For if $y = uvw$; let $vw = z$, then $y = uz$.

Whence
$$\frac{1}{y}\frac{dy}{dx} = \frac{1}{u}\frac{du}{dx} + \frac{1}{z}\frac{dz}{dx}.$$

But
$$\frac{1}{z}\frac{dz}{dx} = \frac{1}{v}\frac{dv}{dx} + \frac{1}{w}\frac{dw}{dx}.$$

Therefore
$$\frac{1}{y}\frac{dy}{dx} = \frac{1}{u}\frac{du}{dx} + \frac{1}{v}\frac{dv}{dx} + \frac{1}{w}\frac{dw}{dx} \quad\dots\dots\dots(5).$$

Multiplying by uvw, we obtain
$$\frac{dy}{dx} = vw\frac{du}{dx} + wu\frac{dv}{dx} + uv\frac{dw}{dx} \quad\dots\dots\dots(6).$$

Similarly for the product of any number of functions.

V. *The differential coefficient of the quotient of two functions is*
$$\frac{(Diff.\ Coeff.\ of\ Numr.)(Denr.) - (Diff.\ Coeff.\ of\ Denr.)(Numr.)}{Square\ of\ Denominator}.$$

Let
$$y = \frac{u}{v}.$$

Then
$$\Delta y = \frac{u + \Delta u}{v + \Delta v} - \frac{u}{v} = \frac{v\Delta u - u\Delta v}{v(v + \Delta v)}$$

and
$$\frac{\Delta y}{\Delta x} = \frac{v\dfrac{\Delta u}{\Delta x} - u\dfrac{\Delta v}{\Delta x}}{v(v + \Delta v)},$$

whence, taking the limit,

$$\frac{dy}{dx} = \frac{v\dfrac{du}{dx} - u\dfrac{dv}{dx}}{v^2} \quad \dots\dots\dots\dots\dots(7),$$

which may be written

$$\frac{1}{y}\frac{dy}{dx} = \frac{1}{u}\frac{du}{dx} - \frac{1}{v}\frac{dv}{dx} \quad \dots\dots\dots\dots(8).$$

VI. *The differential coefficient of y with respect to x, where y is a function of u and u is a function of x, is the product of the differential coefficients of y with respect to u and u with respect to x.*

For
$$\frac{\Delta y}{\Delta x} \equiv \frac{\Delta y}{\Delta u}\cdot\frac{\Delta u}{\Delta x},$$

whence, taking the limit,

$$\frac{dy}{dx} = \frac{dy}{du}\cdot\frac{du}{dx} \quad \dots\dots\dots\dots\dots(9).$$

Similarly
$$\frac{dy}{dx} = \frac{dy}{du}\cdot\frac{du}{dv}\cdot\frac{dv}{dx} \quad \dots\dots\dots\dots(10),$$

and so for any number of functions.

2. Various standard forms can now be developed, mainly from first principles. It is instructive to note the points of analogy with the corresponding forms for Finite Differences.

(i) $\quad y = x^n,$

$$\frac{dy}{dx} = \operatorname*{Lt}_{h\to 0}\frac{(x+h)^n - x^n}{h}$$

$$= \operatorname*{Lt}_{h\to 0}\frac{x^n\left[\left(1+\dfrac{h}{x}\right)^n - 1\right]}{h}$$

Expanding by the Binomial we have

$$\frac{dy}{dx} = \operatorname*{Lt}_{h\to 0}\frac{x^n}{h}\left[n\frac{h}{x} + \binom{n}{2}\frac{h^2}{x^2} + \binom{n}{3}\frac{h^3}{x^3} + \dots\right]$$

$$= \operatorname*{Lt}_{h\to 0} nx^{n-1}\left[1 + \frac{n-1}{2}\frac{h}{x} + \dots\right]$$

$$= nx^{n-1}.$$

(ii) $y = a^x$,

$$\frac{dy}{dx} = \underset{h \to 0}{Lt} \frac{a^{x+h} - a^x}{h}$$

$$= a^x \underset{h \to 0}{Lt} \frac{a^h - 1}{h}$$

$$= a^x \underset{h \to 0}{Lt} \frac{1}{h} \left[1 + h \log_e a + \frac{h^2}{2} (\log_e a)^2 + \ldots - 1 \right]$$

$$= a^x \underset{h \to 0}{Lt} \left[\log_e a + \frac{h}{2} (\log_e a)^2 + \ldots \right]$$

$$= a^x \log_e a.$$

If $\qquad\qquad y = e^x, \quad \dfrac{dy}{dx} = e^x \log_e e = e^x.$

(iii) $\qquad\qquad\qquad\qquad y = \log_a x.$

Then $\qquad\qquad\qquad\qquad a^y = x.$

But $\qquad\qquad\qquad \dfrac{d(a^y)}{dx} = \dfrac{d(a^y)}{dy} \cdot \dfrac{dy}{dx}.$

Hence, using the result established in (ii) and remembering that $a^y = x$, we have

$$\frac{dx}{dx} = a^y \log_e a \cdot \frac{dy}{dx}$$

or $\qquad\qquad\qquad 1 = x \log_e a \cdot \dfrac{dy}{dx}.$

Whence $\qquad\qquad\qquad \dfrac{dy}{dx} = \dfrac{1}{x \log_e a}.$

If $\qquad y = \log_e x, \quad \dfrac{dy}{dx} = \dfrac{1}{x \log_e e} = \dfrac{1}{x}.$

(iv) $\qquad y = [f(x)]^n; \quad y = e^{f(x)}; \quad y = \log_e f(x).$

If $\qquad\qquad\qquad y = [f(x)]^n,$

$$\frac{dy}{dx} = \frac{d[f(x)]^n}{df(x)} \cdot \frac{df(x)}{dx}$$

$$= n[f(x)]^{n-1} \cdot f'(x).$$

Similarly if $\quad y = e^{f(x)}, \quad \dfrac{dy}{dx} = e^{f(x)} \cdot f'(x),$

and if $\qquad y = \log_e f(x), \quad \dfrac{dy}{dx} = \dfrac{f'(x)}{f(x)}.$

(v)
$$y = \sin x,$$
$$\frac{dy}{dx} = \underset{h \to 0}{\text{Lt}} \frac{\sin(x+h) - \sin x}{h}$$
$$= \underset{h \to 0}{\text{Lt}} \frac{2 \sin \frac{h}{2} \cdot \cos\left(x + \frac{h}{2}\right)}{h}$$
$$= \underset{h \to 0}{\text{Lt}} \frac{\sin \frac{h}{2}}{\frac{h}{2}} \cdot \cos\left(x + \frac{h}{2}\right)$$
$$= \cos x.$$

(vi)
$$y = \sin^{-1} x.$$

Then
$$\sin y = x,$$

whence
$$\frac{dx}{dy} = \cos y = \sqrt{1 - \sin^2 y} = \sqrt{1 - x^2}.$$

Therefore
$$\frac{dy}{dx} = \frac{1}{\dfrac{dx}{dy}} = \frac{1}{\sqrt{1 - x^2}}.$$

3. The values of differential coefficients for the other trigonometrical functions can be found by methods similar to those employed in (v) and (vi). The results are given in the table below and should be verified as an exercise by the student.

Function	Differential Coefficient	Function	Differential Coefficient
x^n	$n x^{n-1}$	$\sin^{-1} x$	$\dfrac{1}{\sqrt{1 - x^2}}$
a^x	$a^x \log_e a$		
e^x	e^x	$\cos^{-1} x$	$-\dfrac{1}{\sqrt{1 - x^2}}$
$\log_a x$	$\dfrac{1}{x \log_e a}$	$\tan^{-1} x$	$\dfrac{1}{1 + x^2}$
$\log_e x$	$\dfrac{1}{x}$	$\cot^{-1} x$	$-\dfrac{1}{1 + x^2}$
$\sin x$	$\cos x$		
$\cos x$	$-\sin x$	$\sec^{-1} x$	$\dfrac{1}{x \sqrt{x^2 - 1}}$
$\tan x$	$\sec^2 x$		
$\cot x$	$-\operatorname{cosec}^2 x$	$\operatorname{cosec}^{-1} x$	$-\dfrac{1}{x \sqrt{x^2 - 1}}$
$\sec x$	$\sec x \cdot \tan x$		
$\operatorname{cosec} x$	$-\operatorname{cosec} x \cdot \cot x$		

4. *Logarithmic Differentiation.* This method is of special value in two cases. Thus if $y = uvw \ldots$, where $u, v, w, \ldots$ are functions of x, then

$$\log y = \log u + \log v + \log w + \ldots,$$

and

$$\frac{1}{y}\frac{dy}{dx} = \frac{1}{u}\frac{du}{dx} + \frac{1}{v}\frac{dv}{dx} + \frac{1}{w}\frac{dw}{dx} + \ldots$$

or

$$\frac{dy}{dx} = uvw \left[\frac{1}{u}\frac{du}{dx} + \frac{1}{v}\frac{dv}{dx} + \frac{1}{w}\frac{dw}{dx} + \ldots \right],$$

a result which agrees with that already obtained in § **1**.

Secondly if $y = u^v$, u and v both being functions of x,

$$\log y = v \log u,$$

and

$$\frac{1}{y}\frac{dy}{dx} = \frac{v}{u}\frac{du}{dx} + \log u \frac{dv}{dx}$$

or

$$\frac{dy}{dx} = vu^{v-1}\frac{du}{dx} + u^v \log u \frac{dv}{dx}.$$

5. We will now give some miscellaneous examples of differentiation.

(i)
$$y = \frac{a + x^2}{b + x}.$$

By the ordinary rule for a quotient

$$\frac{dy}{dx} = \frac{(b+x)\dfrac{d\,(a+x^2)}{dx} - (a+x^2)\dfrac{d\,(b+x)}{dx}}{(b+x)^2}$$

$$= \frac{(b+x)\,2x - (a+x^2)}{(b+x)^2} = \frac{x^2 + 2bx - a}{(b+x)^2}.$$

(ii)
$$y = \frac{7x - 1}{1 - 5x + 6x^2}.$$

This can best be treated by resolving the expression into partial fractions. Then

$$y = \frac{4}{1 - 3x} - \frac{5}{1 - 2x},$$

$$\frac{dy}{dx} = 4\,\frac{d\,(1-3x)^{-1}}{d\,(1-3x)}\cdot\frac{d\,(1-3x)}{dx} - 5\,\frac{d\,(1-2x)^{-1}}{d\,(1-2x)}\cdot\frac{d\,(1-2x)}{dx}$$

$$= \frac{12}{(1-3x)^2} - \frac{10}{(1-2x)^2}.$$

(iii) $\qquad y = \sqrt[n]{a + x}.$

$$\frac{dy}{dx} = \frac{d\,(a+x)^{\frac{1}{n}}}{d\,(a+x)} \cdot \frac{d\,(a+x)}{dx} = \frac{1}{n}\,(a+x)^{\frac{1}{n}-1}.$$

(iv) $\qquad y = \log\,(\log x).$

$$\frac{dy}{dx} = \frac{d\,\log\,(\log x)}{d\,(\log x)} \cdot \frac{d\,(\log x)}{dx} = \frac{1}{x\,\log x}.$$

(v) $\qquad y = \tan^{-1}\dfrac{1}{\sqrt{x^2 - 1}}.$

$$\frac{dy}{dx} = \frac{d\left(\tan^{-1}\dfrac{1}{\sqrt{x^2-1}}\right)}{\dfrac{1}{\sqrt{x^2-1}}} \cdot \frac{d\,\dfrac{1}{\sqrt{x^2-1}}}{d\,(x^2-1)} \cdot \frac{d\,(x^2-1)}{dx}$$

$$= \frac{1}{1 + \dfrac{1}{x^2-1}} \cdot -\tfrac{1}{2}\,(x^2-1)^{-\frac{3}{2}}.\,2x$$

$$= -\frac{1}{x\sqrt{x^2-1}}.$$

(vi) $\quad y = \left(\dfrac{x-2}{x-3}\right)^{\frac{1}{x}}.$

$$\log y = \frac{1}{x}\,\log\,\overline{x-2} - \frac{1}{x}\,\log\,\overline{x-3},$$

$$\frac{1}{y}\frac{dy}{dx} = \frac{1}{x}\frac{d\,(\log\,\overline{x-2})}{d\,(x-2)} \cdot \frac{d\,(x-2)}{dx} + \log\,\overline{x-2}\,.\,-\frac{1}{x^2}$$

$$-\,\frac{1}{x}\frac{d\,(\log\,\overline{x-3})}{d\,(x-3)} \cdot \frac{d\,(x-3)}{dx} - \log\,\overline{x-3}\,.\,-\frac{1}{x^2}$$

$$= \frac{1}{x\,(x-2)} - \frac{1}{x\,(x-3)} - \frac{1}{x^2}\log\frac{x-2}{x-3}.$$

Whence $\qquad \dfrac{dy}{dx} = -\left(\dfrac{x-2}{x-3}\right)^{\frac{1}{x}}\left[\dfrac{1}{x\,(x-2)\,(x-3)} + \dfrac{1}{x^2}\log\dfrac{x-2}{x-3}\right].$

(vii) $$y = a^x . b^{c^x}.$$

$$\log y = x \log a + c^x \log b,$$

$$\frac{1}{y}\frac{dy}{dx} = \log a + c^x \log c \log b,$$

$$\frac{dy}{dx} = a^x . b^{c^x} (\log a + c^x \log c \log b).$$

(viii) $$y = x^x + x^{\frac{1}{x}}.$$

In this case logarithmic differentiation must be used, but for this purpose the two terms must be taken separately.

Let $$x^x = u \text{ and } x^{\frac{1}{x}} = v.$$

Then $$\frac{dy}{dx} = \frac{du}{dx} + \frac{dv}{dx},$$

$$\log u = x \log x,$$

$$\frac{1}{u}\frac{du}{dx} = x . \frac{1}{x} + \log x,$$

$$\frac{du}{dx} = x^x (1 + \log x).$$

Also $$\log v = \frac{1}{x} \log x,$$

$$\frac{1}{v}\frac{dv}{dx} = \frac{1}{x} . \frac{1}{x} + \log x . - \frac{1}{x^2},$$

$$\frac{dv}{dx} = x^{\frac{1}{x}} . \frac{1}{x^2} (1 - \log x).$$

Therefore $$\frac{dy}{dx} = x^x (1 + \log x) + x^{\frac{1}{x}-2} (1 - \log x).$$

(ix) Differentiate $\log_e x$ with regard to x^2.

Let $$y = \log_e x \text{ and } z = x^2.$$

Then $$\frac{dy}{dz} = \frac{dy}{dx} . \frac{dx}{dz} = \frac{dy}{dx} . \frac{1}{\frac{dz}{dx}}.$$

Therefore $$\frac{dy}{dz} = \frac{1}{x} . \frac{1}{2x} = \frac{1}{2x^2}.$$

6. In dealing with cases where a function of two variables is involved it is convenient to adopt methods similar to those used in Finite Differences (see Chapter IX, § 4). Thus we define Partial Differentiation as the process of differentiating a function of several variables with reference to any one of them, treating the other variables as constants.

This process is denoted by the symbols $\dfrac{\partial}{\partial x}$, $\dfrac{\partial}{\partial y}$, etc. We will also use the symbol δx to denote a small change in the value of x.

Let $$u = f(x, y).$$
Then $$u + \delta u = f(x + h, y + k)$$
and
$$\delta u = f(x + h, y + k) - f(x, y)$$
$$= \frac{f(x + h, y + k) - f(x, y + k)}{h} \cdot h + \frac{f(x, y + k) - f(x, y)}{k} \cdot k.$$

Proceeding to the limit when h and k successively $\to 0$,

$$\frac{f(x + h, y + k) - f(x, y + k)}{h} = \frac{\partial}{\partial x} f(x, y + k)$$

$$= \frac{\partial}{\partial x} f(x, y), \text{ since } k \to 0.$$

Therefore $$\delta u = \frac{\partial u}{\partial x} \cdot \delta x + \frac{\partial u}{\partial y} \cdot \delta y,$$

and $$\frac{\delta u}{\delta x} = \frac{\partial u}{\partial x} + \frac{\partial u}{\partial y} \cdot \frac{\delta y}{\delta x},$$

or, when $\delta x \to 0$, $$\frac{du}{dx} = \frac{\partial u}{\partial x} + \frac{\partial u}{\partial y} \cdot \frac{dy}{dx} \quad \dots\dots\dots\dots\dots\dots(11).$$

7. If $f(x, y) = 0$, $\dfrac{du}{dx} = 0$ and

$$0 = \frac{\partial u}{\partial x} + \frac{\partial u}{\partial y} \cdot \frac{dy}{dx}.$$

Whence $$\frac{dy}{dx} = -\frac{\dfrac{\partial u}{\partial x}}{\dfrac{\partial u}{\partial y}} \quad \dots\dots\dots\dots\dots\dots(12).$$

Example. If $$x^2 + xy + y^2 = 0,$$

then $$\frac{\partial u}{\partial x} = 2x + y, \quad \frac{\partial u}{\partial y} = x + 2y,$$

and $$\frac{dy}{dx} = -\frac{2x + y}{x + 2y}.$$

CHAPTER XII

DIFFERENTIAL CALCULUS. SUCCESSIVE DIFFERENTIATION

1. When $\frac{dy}{dx}$ is differentiated with respect to x, we obtain a further function of x which is known as the *second differential coefficient* or *second derived function* of y. This operation represented by $\frac{d}{dx}\left(\frac{dy}{dx}\right)$ is generally written $\frac{d^2y}{dx^2}$ or $f''(x)$. If the function is differentiated n times with respect to x, the result is called the nth differential coefficient or nth derived function and is written $\frac{d^ny}{dx^n}$. Other symbols for the nth differential coefficient are $f^{(n)}(x)$, $D^n y$, y_n.

2. In many cases the value of the nth differential coefficient can be found readily by inductive reasoning.

Example 1.

$$y = \log(x+a).$$

$$y_1 = \frac{1}{x+a}; \ y_2 = -\frac{1}{(x+a)^2}; \ y_3 = \frac{(-1)(-2)}{(x+a)^3};$$

and by analogy

$$y_n = (-1)^{n-1}\frac{(n-1)!}{(x+a)^n}.$$

Example 2.

$$y = a + bx + cx^2 + \quad dx^3 + \dots + kx^n,$$

$$y_1 = \quad b + 2cx + \quad 3dx^2 + \dots + n \cdot kx^{n-1},$$

$$y_2 = \quad\quad\quad 2c + 2 \cdot 3dx + \dots + n(n-1)kx^{n-2},$$

$$\vdots \quad\quad\quad\quad\quad \vdots$$

$$y_n = \quad\quad\quad\quad\quad\quad\quad n!k.$$

Example 3.

$$y = \frac{7x-1}{1-5x+6x^2}.$$

Making use of the method of partial fractions,

$$y = \frac{4}{1-3x} - \frac{5}{1-2x};$$

$$y_1 = \frac{4.3}{(1-3x)^2} - \frac{5.2}{(1-2x)^2},$$

$$\vdots \qquad \vdots$$

$$y_n = \frac{4.3^n.n!}{(1-3x)^{n+1}} - \frac{5.2^n.n!}{(1-2x)^{n+1}}.$$

3. Leibnitz's Theorem.

This theorem gives an expression for $\dfrac{d^n y}{dx^n}$, where y is the product of two functions of x, say u and v.

It should be noted first that, as shown in Chapter XI, § 1, the operator $\dfrac{d}{dx}$ or D obeys the distributive and index laws and is commutative in regard to constants. In these respects it is similar to Δ (see Chapter II, § 6).

Now

$$\frac{d}{dx}(uv) = v\frac{du}{dx} + u\frac{dv}{dx};$$

and we may therefore write

$$D(uv) = D_1(uv) + D_2(uv)$$
$$= (D_1 + D_2)uv,$$

where D_1 operates only on u and differential coefficients of u and D_2 operates only on v and differential coefficients of v.

Therefore

$$D^n(uv) = (D_1 + D_2)^n uv$$
$$= \left[D_1{}^n + n D_1{}^{n-1} D_2 + \binom{n}{2} D_1{}^{n-2} D_2{}^2 + \dots + D_2{}^n \right] uv.$$

Now

$$D_1{}^n(uv) = v\frac{d^n u}{dx^n},$$

$$D_1{}^{n-1} D_2(uv) = D_1{}^{n-1}\left(u\frac{dv}{dx} \right) = \frac{dv}{dx} \cdot \frac{d^{n-1} u}{dx^{n-1}},$$

etc.

Hence

$$\frac{d^n(uv)}{dx^n} = v\frac{d^n u}{dx^n} + n\frac{dv}{dx} \cdot \frac{d^{n-1} u}{dx^{n-1}} + \binom{n}{2}\frac{d^2 v}{dx^2} \cdot \frac{d^{n-2} u}{dx^{n-2}} + \dots + u\frac{d^n v}{dx^n}$$

$$\dots\dots\dots(1).$$

This formula can also be established by induction, but the proof by this method is left as an exercise to the student.

4. Examples of the application of the formula are given below.

Example 1. $$y = x^3 e^{ax}.$$

Since $\dfrac{d^n e^{ax}}{dx^n}$ can be written at once as $a^n e^{ax}$, it is convenient to take x^3 as the factor v, and e^{ax} as the factor u.

Then $$\frac{dv}{dx} = 3x^2, \text{ etc.}$$

Therefore

$$y_n = x^3 a^n e^{ax} + n \cdot 3x^2 \cdot a^{n-1} e^{ax} + \binom{n}{2} \cdot 6x \cdot a^{n-2} e^{ax} + \binom{n}{} \cdot 6 \cdot a^{n-3} e^{ax}.$$

Example 2. If $$y = x^n (\log x)^2,$$
prove that
$$x^2 y_{n+2} + x y_{n+1} = 2 \times n!.$$

We have $$y_1 = x^n \cdot \frac{2 \log x}{x} + (\log x)^2 n \cdot x^{n-1}$$

or $$x y_1 = 2x^n \log x + n x^n (\log x)^2$$
$$= 2x^n \log x + ny \quad \dots\dots\dots\dots\dots\text{(i).}$$

Differentiating both sides of the equation

$$x y_2 + y_1 = \frac{2x^n}{x} + 2 \log x \cdot n x^{n-1} + n y_1$$

or $$x^2 y_2 + x y_1 = 2x^n + 2n x^n \log x + n x y_1.$$

Substituting for $x^n \log x$ from equation (i) we obtain

$$x^2 y_2 + x y_1 = 2x^n + n x y_1 - n^2 y + n x y_1$$

or $$x^2 y_2 - (2n - 1) x y_1 + n^2 y = 2x^n \quad \dots\dots\dots\dots\text{(ii).}$$

By differentiating each term of this equation n times, making use of Leibnitz's Theorem, we arrive at the result

$$\frac{\begin{aligned} x^2 y_{n+2} + \qquad n y_{n+1} \cdot 2x + \quad n(n-1) y_n \\ - (2n-1) y_{n+1} \cdot x - n(2n-1) y_n \\ + n^2 y_n \end{aligned}}{x^2 y_{n+2} + x y_{n+1}} = 2 \times n!.$$

CHAPTER XIII

DIFFERENTIAL CALCULUS. EXPANSIONS. TAYLOR'S AND MACLAURIN'S THEOREMS

1. It is often necessary to expand $f(x)$ in a series of ascending powers of x. This has been done by ordinary algebraic or trigonometrical methods in such cases as $(x + a)^n$, e^x, $\log_e (1 + x)$, $\sin x$, etc.

The various methods which can be employed may be summarised as follows:

   I.   By algebraic or trigonometrical methods.

   II. By the use of Taylor's or Maclaurin's Theorem.

   III. By the use of a differential equation.

   IV. By differentiating or integrating a known series. [For integration, see Chapters XVI–XX.]

2. I. An example will make this method sufficiently clear.

Example 1.
$$\frac{1}{e^t - 1} = \frac{1}{t + \dfrac{t^2}{2!} + \dfrac{t^3}{3!} + \dfrac{t^4}{4!} + \dots}$$

$$= \frac{1}{t} - \frac{1}{2} + \frac{t}{12} - \frac{t^3}{720} + \dots$$

by actual division.

3. II. *Taylor's and Maclaurin's Theorems.*

Assume that $f(x + h)$ can be expanded in a series of positive integral powers of h.

Let
$$f(x + h) = a + bh + ch^2 + dh^3 + \dots.$$

Differentiating with regard to h,
$$f'(x + h) = b + 2ch + 3dh^2 + \dots,$$
$$f''(x + h) = \qquad 2c + 3 \cdot 2dh + \dots,$$

and so on.

Put $h = 0$, then we have
$$a = f(x), \quad b = f'(x), \quad c = \frac{f''(x)}{2!}, \text{ etc.}$$

Hence
$$f(x + h) = f(x) + hf'(x) + \frac{h^2}{2!}f''(x) + \frac{h^3}{3!}f'''(x) + \dots + \frac{h^n}{n!}f^{(n)}(x) + \dots.$$

This result is known as **Taylor's Theorem**.

4. If in the above result we put $x = 0$ we obtain

$$f(h) = f(0) + hf'(0) + \frac{h^2}{2!}f''(0) + \ldots + \frac{h^n}{n!}f^{(n)}(0) + \ldots,$$

which, by altering the notation, may be written

$$f(x) = f(0) + xf'(0) + \frac{x^2}{2!}f''(0) + \ldots + \frac{x^n}{n!}f^{(n)}(0) + \ldots.$$

This result is known as Stirling's or Maclaurin's Theorem.

The student should verify the common algebraic and trigonometrical expansions by means of the above theorems.

Example 2.

$$f(x) = \log(1 + e^x), \qquad\qquad f(0) = \log 2,$$

$$f'(x) = \frac{e^x}{1 + e^x} = 1 - \frac{1}{1 + e^x}, \qquad\qquad f'(0) = \tfrac{1}{2},$$

$$f''(x) = \frac{e^x}{(1 + e^x)^2}, \qquad\qquad f''(0) = \tfrac{1}{4},$$

$$f'''(x) = \frac{e^x - e^{2x}}{(1 + e^x)^3}, \qquad\qquad f'''(0) = 0,$$

$$f^{\text{iv}}(x) = \frac{e^x - 4e^{2x} + e^{3x}}{(1 + e^x)^4}, \qquad\qquad f^{\text{iv}}(0) = -\tfrac{1}{8},$$

etc.

Whence, by using Maclaurin's Theorem,

$$\log(1 + e^x) = f(x) = \log 2 + \frac{x}{2} + \frac{x^2}{8} - \frac{x^4}{192} \ldots.$$

5. The above results are not universal in their application. Thus it can be shown that the method fails if $f(x)$ or one of its derivatives becomes infinite or discontinuous between the specified range of values of x. Further, the series obtained must be a convergent series. Lagrange has shown that the remainder after the first n terms have been taken from Taylor's series can be expressed as $\frac{h^n}{n!}f^{(n)}(x + \theta h)$, where θ is a positive proper fraction. The corresponding value of the remainder in the case of Maclaurin's Theorem is $\frac{x^n}{n!}f^{(n)}(\theta x)$. Unless therefore those expressions tend to vanish when n becomes infinite, the series is divergent and the method fails.

6. III. *The use of a differential equation.*

The following are examples of the use of this method.

Example 3.

$$y = (1 + x)^n = a_0 + a_1 x + a_2 x^2 + a_3 x^3 + \ldots .$$

Then $\quad y_1 = n (1 + x)^{n-1}$ or $(1 + x) y_1 = ny.$

Differentiating the first equation,

$$y_1 = a_1 + 2a_2 x + 3a_3 x^2 + \ldots .$$

Therefore

$$(1 + x) (a_1 + 2a_2 x + 3a_3 x^2 + \ldots) \equiv n (a_0 + a_1 x + a_2 x^2 + \ldots).$$

Whence, by comparing coefficients,

$$a_1 = na_0,$$
$$2a_2 + a_1 = na_1,$$
$$3a_3 + 2a_2 = na_2,$$
$$\text{etc.}$$

Putting $x = 0$ in the original equation we have

$$a_0 = 1,$$

and successively

$$a_1 = na_0 \qquad = n,$$

$$a_2 = \frac{(n-1)}{2} a_1 = \frac{n(n-1)}{2!} .$$

$$a_3 = \frac{(n-2)}{3} a_2 = \frac{n(n-1)(n-2)}{3!} ,$$

$$\text{etc.}$$

Hence $\quad (1 + x)^n = 1 + nx + \binom{n}{2} x^2 + \binom{n}{3} x^3 + \ldots .$

Example 4. $\quad y = \sin^{-1} x = a_0 + a_1 x + a_2 x^2 + \ldots ,$

$$y_1 = \frac{1}{\sqrt{1 - x^2}}$$

and $\quad (1 - x^2) y_1^2 = 1.$

Differentiating $\quad (1 - x^2) 2y_1 y_2 - 2xy_1^2 = 0$

or $\quad\quad\quad\quad\quad (1 - x^2) y_2 = xy_1.$

Now $\quad\quad\quad\quad \sin^{-1} x \equiv - \sin^{-1} (- x).$

Therefore

$$a_0 + a_1 x + a_2 x^2 + a_3 x^3 + \ldots \equiv - (a_0 - a_1 x + a_2 x^2 - a_3 x^3 + \ldots).$$

Whence $\quad\quad\quad\quad a_0 = a_2 = a_4 = \ldots = 0.$

Thus we may write

$$y = a_1 x + \quad a_3 x^3 + \ldots + a_{2n+1} x^{2n+1} + \ldots,$$

$$\frac{y}{x} = a_1 + \quad a_3 x^2 + \ldots + a_{2n+1} x^{2n} + \ldots,$$

$$y_1 = a_1 + \quad 3a_3 x^2 + \ldots + \overline{2n+1}\, a_{2n+1} x^{2n} + \ldots,$$

$$y_2 = \quad 3 . 2 a_3 x + \ldots + \overline{2n+1} . 2n . a_{2n+1} x^{2n-1} + \ldots .$$

Therefore

$$(1 - x^2)(3 . 2 . a_3 x + \ldots + \overline{2n+1} . 2n . a_{2n+1} x^{2n-1} + \ldots) \equiv x(a_1 + 3a_3 x^2 + \ldots$$
$$+ \overline{2n+1}\, a_{2n+1} x^{2n} + \ldots).$$

Whence $\qquad a_1 = 3 . 2 a_3,$

$$3a_3 = 5 . 4 a_5 - 3 . 2 a_3,$$

$$\vdots \qquad\qquad \vdots$$

$$(2n+1) a_{2n+1} = (2n+3)(2n+2) a_{2n+3} - (2n+1) 2n . a_{2n+1}$$

or $\quad (2n+1)^2 a_{2n+1} = (2n+3)(2n+2) a_{2n+3}.$

But in the limit when $x \to 0$, $\dfrac{y}{x} = 1$.

Therefore $\qquad\qquad a_1 = 1,$

and accordingly $\qquad a_3 = \dfrac{1}{2 . 3},$

$$a_5 = \dfrac{1 . 3}{2 . 4 . 5},$$

etc.

and $\qquad \sin^{-1} x = x + \dfrac{1}{2} \cdot \dfrac{x^3}{3} + \dfrac{1 . 3}{2 . 4} \cdot \dfrac{x^5}{5} + \ldots .$

7. IV. *Differentiation or integration of a known series.*

The method is sufficiently indicated by the following examples.

Example 5. $\qquad \sin x = x - \dfrac{x^3}{3!} + \dfrac{x^5}{5!} - \ldots,$

$$\dfrac{d \sin x}{dx} = \cos x = 1 - \dfrac{x^2}{2!} + \dfrac{x^4}{4!} - \ldots .$$

We have therefore obtained the expansion of $\cos x$ in terms of x from that of $\sin x$.

Example 6. Let

$$y = \log_e (1 - x) = a_0 + a_1 x + a_2 x^2 + \ldots,$$

$$\frac{dy}{dx} = -\frac{1}{1 - x} = a_1 + 2a_2 x + 3a_3 x^2 + \ldots.$$

But $\qquad \dfrac{1}{1 - x} = 1 + x + x^2 + x^3 + \ldots.$ $\qquad (x < 1)$

Therefore, comparing coefficients,

$$a_1 = -1, \quad a_2 = -\tfrac{1}{2}, \quad a_3 = -\tfrac{1}{3}, \text{ etc.}$$

Also putting $x = 0$ in the original equation, we find $a_0 = 0$.

Hence $\qquad \log_e (1 - x) = -x - \dfrac{x^2}{2} - \dfrac{x^3}{3} - \ldots.$ $\qquad (x < 1)$

Thus our knowledge of the expansion of $\dfrac{1}{1 - x}$ in terms of x enables us to find the expansion of $\log_e (1 - x)$.

CHAPTER XIV

DIFFERENTIAL CALCULUS. MISCELLANEOUS APPLICATIONS

LIMITING VALUES OR UNDETERMINED FORMS

1. In certain cases the value of a function cannot be at once ascertained. A common form is illustrated by $\underset{h \to 1}{\text{Lt}} \dfrac{x^n - 1}{x - 1}$, the value of which is not apparent since it takes the form $\dfrac{0}{0}$. The function in this case is said to take an *Undetermined* or *Indeterminate Form*, and since, in the limit, its value is represented by the ratio of two indefinitely small quantities, it may be expected that the methods of the Differential Calculus will enable the *Limiting Value* of the function to be found.

2. The process to be employed can best be illustrated by examples.

Example 1. To find $\underset{x \to 1}{\text{Lt}} \left[\dfrac{x^n - 1}{x - 1} \right]$.

Let $x = 1 + h$, then

$$\underset{x \to 1}{\text{Lt}} \left[\frac{x^n - 1}{x - 1} \right] = \underset{h \to 0}{\text{Lt}} \left[\frac{(1 + h)^n - 1}{(1 + h) - 1} \right]$$

$$= \underset{h \to 0}{\text{Lt}} \left[\frac{nh + \binom{n}{2} h^2 + \binom{n}{3} h^3 + \ldots}{h} \right]$$

$$= \underset{h \to 0}{\text{Lt}} \left[n + \binom{n}{2} h + \binom{n}{3} h^2 + \ldots \right]$$

$$= n.$$

Example 2. To find $\underset{x \to 0}{\text{Lt}} \left[\dfrac{\log (1 + x)}{e^x - 1} \right]$.

$$\underset{x \to 0}{\text{Lt}} \left[\frac{\log (1 + x)}{e^x - 1} \right] = \underset{x \to 0}{\text{Lt}} \left[\frac{x - \dfrac{x^2}{2} + \dfrac{x^3}{3} - \ldots}{x + \dfrac{x^2}{2!} + \dfrac{x^3}{3!} + \ldots} \right]$$

$$= \underset{x \to 0}{\text{Lt}} \left[1 - x + \frac{2}{3} x^2 - \ldots \right] \text{ (by actual division)}$$

$$= 1,$$

since the series obtained by division is obviously convergent.

Example 3. To find $\quad \underset{x \to 0}{\text{Lt}} \dfrac{g^{c^x} - g}{g^x - 1}$.

$$\underset{x \to 0}{\text{Lt}} \frac{g^{c^x} - g}{g^x - 1} = \underset{x \to 0}{\text{Lt}} \frac{g\,[g^{c^x - 1} - 1]}{g^x - 1}$$

$$= \underset{x \to 0}{\text{Lt}} \frac{g\,[g^{x \log c + \frac{x^2}{2!}(\log c)^2 + \dots} - 1]}{g^x - 1}$$

$$= \underset{x \to 0}{\text{Lt}} \frac{g\left[\left\{x \log c + \dfrac{x^2}{2!}(\log c)^2 + \dots\right\}\log g \right.}{\left. + \left\{x \log c + \dfrac{x^2}{2!}(\log c)^2 + \dots\right\}^2 \dfrac{(\log g)^2}{2!} + \dots\right]}{x \log g + \dfrac{x^2}{2!}(\log g)^2 + \dots}$$

$$= \underset{x \to 0}{\text{Lt}} \frac{g\,x \log g \log c + \text{terms involving } x^2 \text{ and higher powers of } x}{x \log g + \dfrac{x^2}{2!}(\log g)^2 + \dots}$$

$$= \underset{x \to 0}{\text{Lt}} \frac{g \log g \log c + \text{terms involving } x \text{ and higher powers of } x}{\log g + \dfrac{x}{2!}(\log g)^2 + \dots}$$

$$= g \log c.$$

3. The formulas of the Differential Calculus can be used for the solution of problems of this class, in the following way.

Let $\dfrac{f(x)}{\phi(x)}$ take the form $\dfrac{0}{0}$ when $x \to a$.

Then if $x = a + h$, by Taylor's Theorem,

$$\frac{f(x)}{\phi(x)} = \frac{f(a) + hf'(a) + \dots}{\phi(a) + h\phi'(a) + \dots}.$$

Therefore, when $x \to a$, and consequently h, $f(a)$ and $\phi(a)$ all $\to 0$, we have

$$\underset{x \to a}{\text{Lt}} \frac{f(x)}{\phi(x)} = \frac{f'(a)}{\phi'(a)}.$$

If this is still an undetermined form, the process can be repeated. Taking Example 3 above, we have

$$f(x) = g^{c^x} - g, \qquad\qquad \phi(x) = g^x - 1,$$

$$f'(x) = g^{c^x} c^x \log g \log c, \qquad \phi'(x) = g^x \log g.$$

Therefore $\qquad \underset{x \to 0}{\text{Lt}} \dfrac{f(x)}{\phi(x)} = \underset{x \to 0}{\text{Lt}} \dfrac{g^{c^x} c^x \log g \log c}{g^x \log g}$

$$= g \log c, \text{ as before.}$$

4. Other Undetermined Forms are found when a function in the limit assumes one of the following forms :

$$0 \times \infty, \quad \frac{\infty}{\infty}, \quad \infty - \infty, \quad 0^0, \quad \infty^0, \text{ or } 1^\infty.$$

These can all be made to depend upon the form $\dfrac{0}{0}$.

Thus if $f(x)$ and $\phi(x)$ be the two functions involved, in the first case by writing $f(x) \times \phi(x)$ as $\dfrac{f(x)}{[\phi(x)]^{-1}}$ we have the form $\dfrac{0}{0}$ and can proceed as before.

Similarly for the second form.

The third form can be written as $\infty \left\{ 1 - \dfrac{\infty}{\infty} \right\}$; the second term within the bracket can then be evaluated, and the quantity within the bracket will then be found to be zero or otherwise. In the former event the product is of the form $\infty \times 0$ and can be evaluated; in the latter event the value of the product is clearly infinite.

The last three cases are solved by taking logs, when the logarithm of the function will be found to fall within one of the cases already discussed.

5. In connection with the form 1^∞, it is useful to remember that, from the development of the Exponential Theorem in algebra, it follows that

$$\underset{x \to \infty}{\text{Lt}} \left(1 + \frac{1}{x} \right)^x = e$$

and $\qquad\qquad \underset{x \to \infty}{\text{Lt}} \left(1 + \frac{a}{x} \right)^x = e^a.$

MAXIMA AND MINIMA

6. If $f(x)$ continuously increases with x until it attains a certain value a and subsequently decreases, the value a is said to be a maximum value of the function. Conversely if the value of the function continuously decreases, while x increases, until it attains a value b and subsequently increases, the value b is said to be a minimum value.

By this definition there may be several "maximum" values and several "minimum" values; further, a "minimum" value may conceivably be greater than one of the "maximum" values.

These conceptions are illustrated in the following diagram.

Thus the points A and D are maxima, whilst the points B and E are minima. At the point C the value of the function ceases momentarily to increase but is increasing both before and after the point is reached. Such points, where the rate of increase or decrease in the value of the function tends to become constant as the point is reached, are called *points of inflexion*.

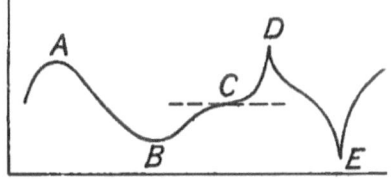

7. In obtaining criteria for ascertaining the maximum or minimum values the following considerations are of importance.

If $f(x)$ increases in value with x, it is clear from the definition that $\frac{dy}{dx}$ is positive. Conversely if $f(x)$ decreases with x, $\frac{dy}{dx}$ is negative.

Further, if $f(x)$ is continuous and assumes two values $f(a)$ and $f(b)$, one of which is positive and the other negative, it follows that for some value of x between the values a and b, $f(x)$ must be either zero or infinite.

8. Now for a maximum value the function increases up to that value and then begins to decrease. Therefore at a maximum value $\frac{dy}{dx}$ must change from positive to negative; similarly at a minimum value $\frac{dy}{dx}$ is changing from negative to positive. It follows from the preceding article that *at a maximum or minimum point the value of $\frac{dy}{dx}$ is zero or infinite.*

9. Further, at a maximum point $\frac{dy}{dx}$ is decreasing from positive to negative, and therefore $\frac{d^2y}{dx^2}$ must be negative or zero. At a minimum point the converse is the case and $\frac{d^2y}{dx^2}$ is positive or zero.

Hence in order to find the maximum and minimum values of $f(x)$ it is necessary

(i) to find the values of x which satisfy the equation $f'(x) = 0$ or $f'(x) = \infty$,

(ii) to ascertain for each of these values whether $f''(x)$ is negative or positive.

If $f''(x) = 0$, a further test is necessary. For the investigation of these cases, which include values which give rise to points of inflexion, the student is referred to more advanced treatises on the subject.

Example 1. What fraction exceeds its pth power by the greatest number possible ?

Let x be the fraction; we have to find the maximum value of

$$y = x - x^p,$$

$$\frac{dy}{dx} = 1 - px^{p-1}.$$

For a maximum or minimum value $\dfrac{dy}{dx} = 0$, therefore

$$1 - px^{p-1} = 0,$$

and

$$x^{p-1} = \frac{1}{p}$$

or

$$x = p^{-\frac{1}{p-1}}.$$

Now

$$\frac{d^2y}{dx^2} = -p(p-1)x^{p-2}$$

$$= -p(p-1)p^{-\frac{p-2}{p-1}},$$

and is therefore negative.

Hence the above value of x is a maximum value.

Example 2. What are the dimensions of the largest rectangular box on a square base the area of whose surface does not exceed 12 square feet ?

Let x be the volume of the box, a the length of the base and b the height.

Then the surface is $2a^2 + 4ab = 12$, whence

$$b = \frac{6 - a^2}{2a}.$$

Also $\qquad\qquad x = a^2 b$

$$= \frac{a^2 (6 - a^2)}{2a} = 3a - \frac{a^3}{2},$$

$$\frac{dx}{da} = 3 - \frac{3a^2}{2},$$

$$\frac{d^2x}{da^2} = -3a.$$

For a maximum or minimum value $\frac{dx}{da} = 0$, therefore

$$3 - \frac{3a^2}{2} = 0$$

or $\qquad\qquad a = \sqrt{2}$, whence $b = \sqrt{2}$,

and since $\frac{d^2x}{da^2}$ is negative when $a = \sqrt{2}$, this value gives a maximum

value for x.

CHAPTER XV

RELATION OF DIFFERENTIAL CALCULUS TO FINITE DIFFERENCES

1. By Taylor's Theorem we have

$$f(x+1) = f(x) + f'(x) + \frac{f''(x)}{2!} + \dots.$$

But $f(x+1) = Ef(x)$, therefore if the operation $\frac{d}{dx}$ be denoted by D we may write symbolically

$$Ef(x) = (1 + D + D^2 + \dots)f(x)$$
$$= e^D f(x)$$

or $\qquad\qquad E = e^D,$

whence $\qquad\qquad \Delta = e^D - 1$

and $\qquad\qquad D = \log_e(1 + \Delta).$

Therefore $\qquad \dfrac{d}{dx} = \Delta - \dfrac{\Delta^2}{2} + \dfrac{\Delta^3}{3} - \dots \qquad\qquad$ ....(1).

If the interval of differencing be h, we have

$$f(x+h) = f(x) + hf'(x) + \frac{h^2}{2!}f''(x) + \dots$$

and therefore $\qquad \Delta = e^{hD} - 1.$

Further, $\qquad\qquad D^2 = [\log_e(1 + \Delta)]^2,$

whence $\qquad \dfrac{d^2y}{dx^2} = \left[\Delta - \dfrac{\Delta^2}{2} + \dfrac{\Delta^3}{3} - \dots\right]^2 y$

$$= \Delta^2 y - \Delta^3 y + \tfrac{11}{12}\Delta^4 y - \tfrac{5}{6}\Delta^5 y + \dots \quad \dots(2).$$

Similarly $\qquad \dfrac{d^3y}{dx^3} = \Delta^3 y - \tfrac{3}{2}\Delta^4 y + \tfrac{7}{4}\Delta^5 y - \dots \qquad$ ....(3).

2. The above formula (1) gives a convenient expression for the differential coefficient in terms of advancing differences. But from the nature of the differential coefficient, it may be expected that a better result will be obtained by applying the formulas of central differences.

Thus, taking Stirling's formula, we have

$$f(x) = f(0) + x\frac{\Delta f(0) + \Delta f(-1)}{2} + \frac{x^2}{2}\Delta^2 f(-1)$$

$$+ \frac{x(x^2-1)}{3!}\frac{\Delta^3 f(-1) + \Delta^3 f(-2)}{2} + \dots$$

Differentiating with regard to x,

$$f'(x) = \frac{\Delta f(0) + \Delta f(-1)}{2} - \frac{\Delta^3 f(-1) + \Delta^3 f(-2)}{12} + \dots$$

$$+ \text{ terms involving } x \text{ and its powers.}$$

Putting $x = 0$ we obtain

$$f'(0) = \frac{\Delta f(0) + \Delta f(-1)}{2} - \frac{\Delta^3 f(-1) + \Delta^3 f(-2)}{12} + \dots \ (4).$$

Taking the first term only, we have

$$f'(0) = \frac{\Delta f(0) + \Delta f(-1)}{2} = \frac{f(1) - f(-1)}{2} \quad \dots\dots(5),$$

a very useful approximation, which, by altering the origin and the unit of measurement, may be expressed more generally as

$$f'(x) = \frac{f(x+h) - f(x-h)}{2h} \quad \dots\dots\dots\dots\dots(6).$$

If $h = \frac{1}{2}$ we arrive at the approximate result

$$f'(x) = \Delta f(x - \tfrac{1}{2}) \ \dots\dots\dots\dots\dots\dots\dots\dots\dots\dots\dots(7)$$

$$= \Delta (1 + \Delta)^{-\frac{1}{2}} f(x)$$

$$= [\Delta - \tfrac{1}{2}\Delta^2 + \tfrac{3}{8}\Delta^3 - \tfrac{5}{16}\Delta^4 + \tfrac{35}{128}\Delta^5 - \dots] f(x).$$

Comparing this with the value given by formula (1) we see that the error involved in taking $f'(x) = \Delta f(x - \frac{1}{2})$ is

$$[-\tfrac{1}{24}\Delta^3 + \tfrac{1}{16}\Delta^4 - \tfrac{47}{640}\Delta^5 + \dots] f(x),$$

which is approximately equal to $- \tfrac{1}{24}\Delta^3 f(x - \tfrac{3}{2})$.

Hence we may write

$$f'(x) = \Delta f(x - \tfrac{1}{2}) - \tfrac{1}{24}\Delta^3 f(x - \tfrac{3}{2}) \ \dots\dots\dots\dots(8).$$

3. The introduction of the second term in equation (4) gives the useful approximation

$$f'(0) = \frac{8\{f(1) - f(-1)\} - \{f(2) - f(-2)\}}{12} \quad \dots\dots(9).$$

The other formulas of central differences, when treated as above, give these and other expressions for $f'(x)$. The above, however, are the most accurate and useful for general use.

4. Using the central difference formula, we shall obtain for the differential coefficients of higher orders,

$$f''(0) = \Delta^2 f(-1) - \tfrac{1}{12}\Delta^4 f(-2) \quad \ldots\ldots\ldots\ldots(10)$$

and
$$f'''(0) = \frac{\Delta^3 f(-1) + \Delta^3 f(-2)}{2}$$

$$= \Delta^3 f(-\tfrac{3}{2}) \text{ approx.} \quad \ldots\ldots\ldots\ldots\ldots(11).$$

5. An example of the working of the above formulas is now given.

Example. Find the first three differential coefficients of $\log x$, when $x = 2$. having given the values of $\log_e 1\cdot80$, $\log_e 1\cdot90$, ...

Number	Natural log	Δ	Δ²	Δ³	Δ⁴	Δ⁵
1·80	·587787	·054067	− ·002774	·000271	− ·000038	·000007
1·90	·641854	·051293	− ·002503	·000233	− ·000031	·000005
2·00	·693147	·048790	− ·002270	·000202	− ·000026	·000004
2·10	·741937	·046520	− ·002068	·000176	− ·000022	·000004
2·20	·788457	·044452	− ·001892	·000154	− ·000018	
2·30	·832909	·042560	− ·001738	·000136		
2·40	·875469	·040822	− ·001602			
2·50	·916291	·039220				
2·60	·955511					

Using the advancing difference formula (1), starting at the term 2·00, and remembering that the interval of differencing is not unity but ·1, we get

$$f'(x) = 10 \left(·048790 + \frac{·002270}{2} + \frac{·000202}{3} + \frac{·000026}{4} + \frac{·000004}{5} \right)$$
$$= ·50000.$$

Similarly

$$f''(x) = 100 \left(- ·002270 - ·000202 - \tfrac{11}{12} \times ·000026 - \tfrac{5}{6} \times ·000004 \right)$$
$$= - ·2499,$$

$$f'''(x) = 1000 \left(·000202 + \tfrac{3}{2} \times ·000026 + \tfrac{7}{4} \times ·000004 \right)$$
$$= ·248.$$

The true values are, of course, given by the differential coefficients of $\log x$, which are respectively $\dfrac{1}{x}$, $-\dfrac{1}{x^2}$, $\dfrac{2}{x^3}$. When $x = 2$ these become $\tfrac{1}{2}$, $-\tfrac{1}{4}$, $\tfrac{1}{4}$; the closeness of the above approximations is apparent.

Formulas (6) and (9) give respectively for $f'(x)$ values of ·50042 and ·50000.

CHAPTER XVI

INTEGRAL CALCULUS. DEFINITIONS AND ILLUSTRATIONS

1. In Finite Differences we discussed under the heading of Finite Integration the problem of finding the value of $f(0) + f(1) + \ldots + f(n-1)$, or, changing the origin and the unit of measurement, the more general series

$$h[f(a) + f(a+h) + f(a+2h) + \ldots + f(a + \overline{n-1}h)].$$

The Integral Calculus deals with the value which this summation assumes when h becomes indefinitely small.

2. Now let $F(x)$ be a function such that $f(x)$ is its differential coefficient. Then by definition

$$f(a) = \operatorname{Lt}_{h \to 0} \frac{F(a+h) - F(a)}{h}$$

or

$$f(a) = \frac{F(a+h) - F(a)}{h} + \alpha_1,$$

where α_1 is a quantity that vanishes when $h \to 0$.

Then we have

$$hf(a) = F(a+h) - F(a) + h\alpha_1,$$
$$hf(a+h) = F(a+2h) - F(a+h) + h\alpha_2,$$
$$hf(a+2h) = F(a+3h) - F(a+2h) + h\alpha_3,$$
$$\vdots \qquad \vdots \qquad \vdots \qquad \vdots$$
$$hf(a + \overline{n-1}h) = F(a+nh) - F(a + \overline{n-1}h) + h\alpha_n.$$

By addition,

$$h[f(a) + f(a+h) + f(a+2h) + \ldots + f(a + \overline{n-1}h)]$$
$$= F(a+nh) - F(a) + h[\alpha_1 + \alpha_2 + \ldots + \alpha_n].$$

Now if α denote the greatest of the quantities $\alpha_1, \alpha_2, \ldots \alpha_n$, the last term is clearly less than $nh\alpha$, or $(b-a)\alpha$, if $a + nh$ be put equal to b. This term therefore vanishes in the limit and we are left with the relation

$$\operatorname{Lt}_{h \to 0} h[f(a) + f(a+h) + \ldots + f(b-h)] = F(b) - F(a).$$

This result is usually expressed in the form

$$\int_a^b f(x)\, dx = F(b) - F(a),$$

where $F(x)$ is a quantity such that $f(x)$ is its differential coefficient and dx represents, in the limit, the indefinitely small interval between the terms which are summed.

The expression $\int_a^b f(x)\, dx$ is called the *definite integral* of $f(x)$ with regard to x, and b and a are called respectively the *superior* and *inferior* limits of integration.

Where no limits to the summation are expressed and we are concerned merely with the form of the function, we obtain the *indefinite integral*.

3. A geometrical illustration of the process of integration may be obtained as follows.

Let the equation $y = f(x)$ be represented by the curve in the diagram. Let $OA = a$ and $OB = b$, so that $MA = f(a)$ and $NB = f(b)$.

Further, let AB be divided into n parts each equal to h. Then the sum of the rectangles shown is clearly equal to $\sum\limits_{x=a+h}^{x=b} h f(x)$, and, in the limit, when $h \to 0$ the value of the integral becomes equal to the area between the curve and the axis of x bounded by the ordinates MA and NB.

CHAPTER XVII

INTEGRAL CALCULUS. STANDARD FORMS

1. In the preceding chapter we found that the process of integration is the converse of that of differentiation. In other words, that given $f'(x)$ we have to find a function $f(x)$ such that $f'(x)$ is its first differential coefficient. The analogy with the process of finite integration is apparent and the remarks made in Chapter VII, §5, apply equally to the present case.

It may, therefore, be said again that the process of integration cannot be carried out for every function, that definite rules cannot be laid down to apply in every case, and that the student must look to applying the results of the differential calculus as a guide in solving any problem presented by the function under consideration.

2. In the first place it is necessary to point out that the ordinary algebraic laws apply to the integrating symbol $\int dx$ in the same way as they have been shown to apply to the symbolic operations Δ and $\dfrac{d}{dx}$. Thus:

(1) The operation is distributive for, if $u, v, w, \ldots$ be any functions of x,

$$\frac{d}{dx}\left\{\int u\,dx + \int v\,dx + \int w\,dx + \ldots\right\} = u + v + w \ldots$$

and therefore

$$\int u\,dx + \int v\,dx + \int w\,dx + \ldots = \int (u + v + w + \ldots)\,dx \quad \ldots(1).$$

(2) The operation is commutative with regard to constants, for,

if $\dfrac{dv}{dx} = u,$ $\qquad \dfrac{d(cv)}{dx} = \dfrac{c\,dv}{dx} = cu,$

therefore $\qquad \int cu\,dx = cv = c\int u\,dx \quad \ldots\ldots\ldots\ldots\ldots\ldots(2).$

3. It should be added that the process of integration introduces a constant into every indefinite integral, for, if $u = \dfrac{dv}{dx}$:

$$\frac{d(v+c)}{dx} = \frac{dv}{dx} = u,$$

and therefore $\qquad\int u\,dx = v + c,$

which result is, indeed, obvious from the consideration that a constant term disappears on differentiation.

4. In accordance with the symbolic notation which has been previously developed (Chapter XV, § 1), we may write

$$\int f(x)\,dx = \left(\frac{d}{dx}\right)^{-1} f(x) \quad\ldots\ldots\ldots\ldots\ldots\ldots(3)$$

$$= D^{-1} f(x)$$

$$= \left[\frac{1}{\log_e(1+\Delta)}\right] f(x) \quad\ldots\ldots\ldots(4).$$

5. *Standard Forms.*

(a) x^n. Since $\qquad \dfrac{d\left(\dfrac{x^{n+1}}{n+1}\right)}{dx} = \dfrac{(n+1)x^n}{n+1} = x^n,$

therefore $\qquad \int x^n\,dx = \dfrac{x^{n+1}}{n+1} + c.$

(b) x^{-1}. Since $\qquad \dfrac{d(\log x)}{dx} = \dfrac{1}{x},$

therefore $\qquad \int \dfrac{dx}{x} = \log x + c.$

(c) e^x. Since $\qquad \dfrac{d(e^x)}{dx} = e^x,$

therefore $\qquad \int e^x dx = e^x + c.$

(d) a^x. Since $\qquad \dfrac{d\left(\dfrac{a^x}{\log_e a}\right)}{dx} = \dfrac{a^x \log_e a}{\log_e a} = a^x,$

therefore $\qquad \int a^x dx = \dfrac{a^x}{\log_e a} + c.$

Other integrals may be obtained from a consideration of the table of standard forms of differential coefficients given in Chapter XI,

§ 3. The results are embodied in the following table. Their verification is left as an exercise to the student.

Function	Integral
$\int x^n \, dx$	$\dfrac{x^{n+1}}{n+1}$
$\int \dfrac{1}{x} \, dx$	$\log_e x$
$\int a^x \, dx$	$\dfrac{a^x}{\log_e a}$
$\int e^x \, dx$	e^x
$\int \cos x \, dx$	$\sin x$
$\int \sin x \, dx$	$-\cos x$
$\int \sec^2 x \, dx$	$\tan x$
$\int \operatorname{cosec}^2 x \, dx$	$-\cot x$

In each case the constant c has been omitted for the sake of simplicity, but its importance in the result must not be forgotten.

6. Sums of the above functions can be integrated by the use of the distributive property of the operation of integration. Thus

$$\int (x + 2^x) \, dx = \int x^{\frac{5}{2}} \, dx + \int 2^x \, dx$$

$$= \tfrac{2}{7} x^{\frac{7}{2}} + \frac{2^x}{\log_e 2} + c.$$

Similarly $\displaystyle \int (ax^4 + bx^{-4}) \, dx = a \int x^4 \, dx + b \int x^{-4} \, dx$

$$= \frac{ax^5}{5} - \frac{bx^{-3}}{3} + c.$$

7. The problem of integration may be presented in another way. Thus to find the sum of

$$\frac{1}{x} + \frac{1}{x+m} + \frac{1}{x+2m} + \ldots + \frac{1}{x+xm}$$

when x is indefinitely increased.

The series may be written as

$$\frac{1}{m}\left[\frac{1}{1}+\frac{1}{1+\frac{m}{x}}+\frac{1}{1+\frac{2m}{x}}+\ldots+\frac{1}{1+x\cdot\frac{m}{x}}\right]\frac{m}{x}.$$

The terms in the denominator consist of values of a quantity, which can be represented by y, increasing by equal increments of $\frac{m}{x}$. Also the sum of the series is multiplied by $\frac{m}{x}$, which is the increment in the value of the denominator.

Since the initial value of the denominator y is unity and the final value is $1+m$, from our definition of an integral we may write, when $x\to\infty$ and therefore $\frac{m}{x}\to 0$,

$$\underset{x\to\infty}{\mathrm{Lt}}\ \frac{1}{m}\left[\frac{1}{1}+\frac{1}{1+\frac{m}{x}}+\frac{1}{1+\frac{2m}{x}}+\ldots+\frac{1}{1+x\cdot\frac{m}{x}}\right]\frac{m}{x}=\frac{1}{m}\int_{1}^{1+m}\frac{dy}{y}$$

$$=\frac{1}{m}\left[\log y\right]_{1}^{1+m}$$

$$=\frac{1}{m}\log\overline{1+m}.$$

CHAPTER XVIII

INTEGRAL CALCULUS. METHODS OF INTEGRATION

I. The Method of Substitution

1. Various methods are available for treating the integration of functions which are not among the standard forms. Of these methods, one of the most important and most easily applied is the method of substitution. By this method the independent variable x is changed to y where y is a function of x. Thus an integral in terms of y can be obtained which can frequently be made to assume a standard form.

For suppose
$$y = F(x).$$
Then
$$dy = F'(x)\, dx.$$

So that if the original integral is of the form $\int f[F(x)] F'(x)\, dx$, it can be expressed as $\int f(y)\, dy$, which may be a standard form.

No general rules can be given, but the following examples will indicate methods which can frequently be employed with advantage.

2. (1)
$$\int (a + bx)^n \, dx.$$

Put
$$a + bx = y.$$
Then
$$b\, dx = dy.$$

Therefore
$$\int (a + bx)^n \, dx = \int \frac{y^n}{b}\, dy = \frac{y^{n+1}}{(n+1)\, b} + c = \frac{(a+bx)^{n+1}}{(n+1)\, b} + c.$$

(2)
$$\int \frac{x^2\, dx}{(a + bx)^n}.$$

Put
$$a + bx = y.$$
Therefore
$$\int \frac{x^2\, dx}{(a + bx)^n} = \int \frac{(y - a)^2\, dy}{b^3 y^n}$$
$$= \frac{1}{b^3} \int (y^{2-n} - 2a y^{1-n} + a^2 y^{-n})\, dy$$
$$= -\frac{1}{b^3} \left[\frac{1}{(n-3)\, y^{n-3}} - \frac{2a}{(n-2)\, y^{n-2}} + \frac{a^2}{(n-1)\, y^{n-1}} \right] + c$$
where $y = a + bx$.

(3) $$\int (b + 2cx)\,(a + bx + cx^2)^n\,dx.$$

Put $$a + bx + cx^2 = y.$$

Then. $$(b + 2cx)\,dx = dy.$$

Therefore

$$\int (b + 2cx)\,(a + bx + cx^2)^n\,dx = \int y^n\,dy = \frac{y^{n+1}}{n+1} + k$$

$$= \frac{(a + bx + cx^2)^{n+1}}{n+1} + k.$$

(4) $$\int \frac{(\log x)^n\,dx}{x}.$$

Put $$\log x = y.$$

Then $$\frac{1}{x}\,dx = dy.$$

Therefore

$$\int \frac{(\log x)^n\,dx}{x} = \int y^n\,dy = \frac{y^{n+1}}{n+1} + c = \frac{(\log x)^{n+1}}{n+1} + c.$$

(5) $$\int \frac{f'(x)\,dx}{f(x)}.$$

Put $$f(x) = y.$$

Then $$f'(x)\,dx = dy.$$

Therefore

$$\int \frac{f'(x)\,dx}{f(x)} = \int \frac{dy}{y} = \log y + c = \log\,[f(x)] + c.$$

(6) $$\int \frac{x^3\,dx}{1 + x^2}.$$

Put $$x^2 = y.$$

Then $$2x\,dx = dy.$$

Therefore $$\int \frac{x^3\,dx}{1 + x^2} = \tfrac{1}{2}\int \frac{y\,dy}{1 + y} = \tfrac{1}{2}\int \left(1 - \frac{1}{1 + y}\right) dy$$

$$= \tfrac{1}{2}\left[\int dy - \int \frac{dy}{1 + y}\right]$$

$$= \tfrac{1}{2}\left[\int dy - \int \frac{d\,(1 + y)}{1 + y}\right]$$

$$= \tfrac{1}{2}\,[y - \log \overline{1 + y}] + c$$

$$= \tfrac{1}{2}\,[x^2 - \log \overline{1 + x^2}] + c.$$

(7)
$$\int \frac{\sin x \, dx}{a + b \cos x}.$$

Put
$$a + b \cos x = y.$$

Then
$$- b \sin x \, dx = dy.$$

Therefore

$$\int \frac{\sin x \, dx}{a + b \cos x} = - \frac{1}{b} \int \frac{dy}{y} = - \frac{1}{b} \log y + c = - \frac{\log (a + b \cos x)}{b} + c.$$

(8)
$$\int \frac{dx}{\sin x} = \int \frac{dx}{2 \sin \frac{x}{2} \cos \frac{x}{2}}.$$

$$= \int \frac{\sec^2 \frac{x}{2} \, dx}{2 \tan \frac{x}{2}}.$$

Put
$$\tan \frac{x}{2} = y.$$

Then
$$\tfrac{1}{2} \sec^2 \frac{x}{2} \, dx = dy.$$

Therefore
$$\int \frac{dx}{\sin x} = \int \frac{dy}{y} = \log y + c$$
$$= \log \tan \frac{x}{2} + c.$$

Corollary. Since
$$\cos x = \sin \left(\frac{\pi}{2} + x \right),$$
$$\int \frac{dx}{\cos x} = \log \tan \left(\frac{\pi}{4} + \frac{x}{2} \right) + c.$$

II. RATIONALISATION BY TRIGONOMETRICAL TRANSFORMATION

3. The above methods can be extended by the use of trigono-metrical functions and the relations which exist between them.

The following are examples:

(1)
$$\int \frac{dx}{\sqrt{a^2 - x^2}}.$$

Let
$$x = a \sin y.$$

Then
$$dx = a \cos y \, dy,$$

and
$$\sqrt{a^2 - x^2} = a \cos y.$$

Therefore
$$\int \frac{dx}{\sqrt{a^2 - x^2}} = \int dy = y + c$$

$$= \sin^{-1} \frac{x}{a} + c.$$

(2)
$$\int \frac{dx}{\sqrt{x^2 - a^2}}.$$

Let
$$x = a \sec y.$$

Then
$$dx = a \sec y \tan y \, dy,$$

and
$$\sqrt{x^2 - a^2} = a \tan y.$$

Therefore
$$\int \frac{dx}{\sqrt{x^2 - a^2}} = \int \frac{dy}{\cos y} = \log \tan \left(\frac{\pi}{4} + \frac{y}{2} \right) + c$$

$$= \log \frac{1 + \tan \frac{y}{2}}{1 - \tan \frac{y}{2}} + c$$

$$= \log \frac{1 + \sin y}{\cos y} + c$$

$$= \log \frac{1 + \sqrt{1 - \frac{a^2}{x^2}}}{\frac{a}{x}} + c$$

$$= \log \left(\frac{x + \sqrt{x^2 - a^2}}{a} \right) + c.$$

(3)
$$\int \frac{dx}{\sqrt{x^2 + a^2}}.$$

Let
$$x = a \tan y.$$

Then
$$dx = a \sec^2 y \, dy,$$

and
$$\sqrt{x^2 + a^2} = a \sec y.$$

Therefore
$$\int \frac{dx}{\sqrt{x^2 + a^2}} = \int \frac{dy}{\cos y} = \log \tan \left(\frac{\pi}{4} + \frac{y}{2} \right) + c$$

$$= \log (\sec y + \tan y) + c \quad \text{[See Ex. (2)]}$$

$$= \log \left(\frac{x + \sqrt{x^2 + a^2}}{a} \right) + c.$$

From the above integral, two other important forms can be obtained.

(4)
$$\int \frac{dx}{\sqrt{a + 2bx + cx^2}}.$$

This can be written as

$$\int \frac{dx}{\sqrt{\dfrac{(cx + b)^2 + ac - b^2}{c}}} = \int \frac{d\,(cx + b)}{\sqrt{c\,\{(cx + b)^2 + ac - b^2\}}}.$$

Disregarding for the moment the constant multiplier, this can clearly be transformed into one of the forms given in Examples (1)—(3) above.

Corollary. Since

$$\int \frac{dx}{\sqrt{(x - a)(x - b)}} = 2 \log (\sqrt{x - a} + \sqrt{x - b}) + c,$$

$$\int \frac{dx}{\sqrt{(x - a)(b - x)}} = 2 \sin^{-1} \sqrt{\frac{x - a}{b - a}} + c.$$

(5)
$$\int \frac{(p + qx)\,dx}{\sqrt{a + 2bx + cx^2}} = \int \frac{\left[\dfrac{q}{c}(b + cx) + \dfrac{(pc - qb)}{c} \right]}{\sqrt{a + 2bx + cx^2}} \, dx$$

$$= \frac{q}{2c} \int \frac{d\,(a + 2bx + cx^2)}{\sqrt{a + 2bx + cx^2}} + \frac{(pc - qb)}{c} \int \frac{dx}{\sqrt{a + 2bx + cx^2}}.$$

The value of the first integral is $2\,(a + 2bx + cx^2)^{\frac{1}{2}}$ and the second integral can be dealt with as in Example (4).

4. General remarks in regard to the method of substitution. When the precise substitution which will enable the integral to be solved is not apparent the device illustrated in the following examples is often of assistance.

(1)
$$\int \frac{(x + a)\,dx}{(x + b)\sqrt{x + c}}.$$

The appropriate substitution is not apparent, so assume

$$\sqrt{x + c} = y^r,$$

where r may have any value, to be determined subsequently.

Then
$$x + c = y^{2r}$$

and
$$dx = 2r y^{2r-1} dy.$$

The integral thus becomes

$$\int \frac{(y^{2r} + a - c)\, 2r y^{2r-1} dy}{(y^{2r} + b - c)\, y^r}.$$

Clearly this integral can be evaluated if $y^r = y^{2r-1}$, i.e. if $r = 1$, when we get

$$\int 2 \frac{(y^2 + a - c)}{(y^2 + b - c)}\, dy = 2 \int \left[1 + \frac{(a - b)}{(y^2 + b - c)} \right] dy$$

$$= 2y + \int \frac{(a - b)}{\sqrt{c - b}} \left[\frac{1}{y - \sqrt{c - b}} - \frac{1}{y + \sqrt{c - b}} \right] dy$$

$$= 2y + \frac{a - b}{\sqrt{c - b}} \log \frac{y - \sqrt{c - b}}{y + \sqrt{c - b}} + k,$$

where $y = \sqrt{x + c}$.

(2)
$$\int \frac{dx}{(x - p)\sqrt{(a + 2bx + cx^2)}}.$$

Let us take the linear function as likely to lead to simpler results and, as before, put

$$x - p = y^r$$

so that
$$dx = r y^{r-1} dy.$$

Then the transformed integral is

$$\int \frac{r y^{r-1} dy}{y^r \sqrt{a + 2b\,(y^r + p) + c\,(y^r + p)^2}} = \int \frac{r\, dy}{y \sqrt{a + 2b\,(y^r + p) + c\,(y^r + p)^2}}.$$

Obviously if $r = -1$, the denominator reduces to the form

$$\sqrt{a' + 2b'y + c'y^2}$$

and the expression can be immediately integrated.

(3)
$$\int \frac{dx}{(a + cx^2)^{\frac{3}{2}}}.$$

This example is a little more difficult than the two previous ones. As before, let $x = y^r$, so that $dx = r y^{r-1} dy$. Then we have

$$\int \frac{dx}{(a + cx^2)^{\frac{3}{2}}} = \int \frac{r y^{r-1} dy}{(a + cy^{2r})^{\frac{3}{2}}}.$$

The expression within the brackets in the denominator is of an even degree in y, so we will express the integral in the form

$$\int \frac{ry^{r-2}\,d(y^2)}{2(a+cy^{2r})^{\frac{2}{3}}} = \int \frac{ry^{r-2}\,d(y^2)}{2y^{3r}(ay^{-2r}+c)^{\frac{2}{3}}}.$$

This can clearly be integrated if $r-2=3r$, when $r=-1$. The integral then becomes

$$-\frac{1}{2}\int \frac{dy^2}{(ay^2+c)^{\frac{3}{2}}} = -\frac{1}{2a}\int \frac{d(ay^2+c)}{(ay^2+c)^{\frac{3}{2}}} = \frac{1}{a(ay^2+c)^{\frac{1}{2}}}+k$$

$$= \frac{x}{a(a+cx^2)^{\frac{1}{2}}}+k.$$

5. *Definite Integrals.* The above examples of the application of the method of substitution all relate to indefinite integrals and the final form of the indefinite integral is expressed, in each case, in terms of x.

In the case of a definite integral, a step may be saved in the operation by avoiding the final substitution of x in terms of y, provided appropriate changes are made in the values of the limits of integration. An example will make the point clear.

Example. $\displaystyle\int_0^2 \frac{x\,dx}{\sqrt{1+x^2}}.$

Put $x^2 = y.$

Then $2x\,dx = dy.$

Also when $x=0$, $y=0$ and when $x=2$, $y=4$.
Thus we get

$$\int_0^2 \frac{x\,dx}{\sqrt{1+x^2}} = \int_0^4 \frac{dy}{2\sqrt{1+y}} = \left[\sqrt{1+y}\right]_0^4 = \sqrt{5}-1.$$

III. INTEGRATION BY PARTS

6. From the Differential Calculus we have

$$\frac{d(uv)}{dx} = u\frac{dv}{dx} + v\frac{du}{dx}.$$

Whence, by integration,

$$uv = \int u\frac{dv}{dx}\,dx + \int v\frac{du}{dx}\,dx,$$

or
$$\int u \frac{dv}{dx}\, dx = uv - \int v \frac{du}{dx}\, dx.$$

Consequently an integral of a function of the form $u\dfrac{dv}{dx}$ can always be made to depend upon that of a function of the form $v\dfrac{du}{dx}$. The latter may prove to be a standard form and the use of the formula given above may enable an apparently intractable expression to be integrated at once.

The advantage of the method is best exhibited by applying it to a few elementary cases.

(1)
$$\int x \log x\, dx = \frac{1}{2}\int \log x\, \frac{d\,(x^2)}{dx}\, dx$$

$$= \frac{1}{2}\left[x^2 \log x - \int x^2 \frac{d\,(\log x)}{dx}\, dx \right]$$

$$= \frac{1}{2} x^2 \log x - \frac{1}{2}\int x\, dx$$

$$= \frac{1}{2} x^2 \log x - \frac{x^2}{4} + c.$$

(2)
$$\int x\, e^{ax}\, dx = \frac{1}{a}\int x\, \frac{d\, e^{ax}}{dx}\, dx$$

$$= \frac{1}{a}\left[x\, e^{ax} - \int e^{ax} \frac{dx}{dx}\, dx \right]$$

$$= \frac{1}{a}\left[x\, e^{ax} - \frac{e^{ax}}{a} \right] + c.$$

(3)
$$\int \sin^{-1} x\, dx = \int \sin^{-1} x\, \frac{dx}{dx}\, dx$$

$$= x \sin^{-1} x - \int x\, \frac{d\,(\sin^{-1} x)}{dx}\, dx$$

$$= x \sin^{-1} x - \int \frac{x\, dx}{\sqrt{1 - x^2}}$$

$$= x \sin^{-1} x + \frac{1}{2}\int \frac{d\,(1 - x^2)}{\sqrt{1 - x^2}}$$

$$= x \sin^{-1} x + \sqrt{1 - x^2} + c.$$

$$(4) \qquad \int \sqrt{a^2 + x^2}\, dx = \int \sqrt{a^2 + x^2}\, \frac{dx}{dx}\, dx$$

$$= x\sqrt{a^2 + x^2} - \int x\, \frac{d\sqrt{a^2 + x^2}}{dx}\, dx$$

$$= x\sqrt{a^2 + x^2} - \int \frac{x^2 dx}{\sqrt{a^2 + x^2}}$$

$$= x\sqrt{a^2 + x^2} - \int \left[\sqrt{a^2 + x^2} - \frac{a^2}{\sqrt{a^2 + x^2}} \right] dx$$

$$= x\sqrt{a^2 + x^2} - \int \sqrt{a^2 + x^2}\, dx + \int \frac{a^2 dx}{\sqrt{a^2 + x^2}}.$$

Therefore $\quad 2\int \sqrt{a^2 + x^2}\, dx = x\sqrt{a^2 + x^2} + a^2 \log\left[x + \sqrt{a^2 + x^2}\right] + c,$

and $\qquad \int \sqrt{a^2 + x^2}\, dx = \frac{x}{2} \sqrt{a^2 + x^2} + \frac{a^2}{2} \log\left[x + \sqrt{a^2 + x^2}\right] + \frac{c}{2}.$

$$(5) \quad \int \log\left(x + \sqrt{x^2 + a^2}\right) dx = \int \log\left(x + \sqrt{x^2 + a^2}\right) \frac{dx}{dx}\, dx$$

$$= x \log\left(x + \sqrt{x^2 + a^2}\right) - \int x\, \frac{d \log\left(x + \sqrt{x^2 + a^2}\right)}{dx}\, dx$$

$$= x \log\left(x + \sqrt{x^2 + a^2}\right) - \int \frac{x\, dx}{\sqrt{x^2 + a^2}}$$

$$= x \log\left(x + \sqrt{x^2 + a^2}\right) - \sqrt{x^2 + a^2} + c.$$

7. The above process can be expressed in a general form as follows:

$$\int u_t v_t\, dt = \int u_t \frac{d\left(\int v_t dt\right)}{dt}\, dt$$

$$= u_t \int v_t dt - \int \frac{du_t}{dt} \left(\int v_t dt \right) dt.$$

To apply this formula to the definite integral $\int_a^b u_t v_t dt$, we can write $\int v_t dt$ as $\int_a^t v_k dk$, the upper limit being taken as t since the integral must itself be a function of t.

Thus we get

$$\int_a^b u_t v_t \, dt = {}^b\!\left[u_t \int_a^t v_k \, dk - \int \frac{du_t}{dt} \left(\int_a^t v_k \, dk \right) dt \right]$$

$$= u_b \int_a^b v_k \, dk - u_a \int_a^a v_k \, dk - \int_a^b \frac{du_t}{dt} \left(\int_a^t v_k \, dk \right) dt$$

$$= u_b \int_a^b v_k \, dk - \int_a^b \frac{du_t}{dt} \left(\int_a^t v_k \, dk \right) dt,$$

since $\int_a^a v_k \, dk = 0$.

Alternatively, if we express $\int v_t \, dt$ as the definite integral $-\int_t^b v_k \, dk$, we obtain

$$\int_a^b u_t v_t \, dt = u_b \int_a^b v_k \, dk + \int_a^b \frac{du_t}{dt} \left(\int_t^b v_k \, dk \right) dt^*.$$

8. Reduction Formulas. Where integration by parts is not immediately successful, continuation of the operation may ultimately lead to the evaluation of the integral.

Thus $\displaystyle \int x^2 e^x \, dx = \int x^2 \frac{de^x}{dx} \, dx = x^2 e^x - \int e^x \frac{dx^2}{dx} \, dx$

$$= x^2 e^x - 2 \int e^x x \, dx$$

$$= x^2 e^x - 2 \int x \frac{de^x}{dx} \, dx$$

$$= x^2 e^x - 2 \left(x e^x - \int e^x \, dx \right)$$

$$= x^2 e^x - 2x e^x + 2 e^x + c.$$

9. The above case is an example of a Reduction Formula, this designation being used since the application of the method of Integration by Parts effects the reduction by successive steps of one term in the integral.

Thus

$$\int x^m (1-x)^n \, dx = \frac{x^{m+1}(1-x)^n}{m+1} + \int \frac{x^{m+1}}{m+1} n (1-x)^{n-1} \, dx.$$

* See *J.I.A.* Vol. 44, pp. 402–409.

Thus the degree of the term $(1-x)^n$ has been reduced by unity. Successive applications of the formula will reduce the degree further, until, if n is an integer, the term ultimately equals $(1-x)^0$ or unity.

In the special case where the value of this integral is taken between the limits 0 and 1, we have

$$\int_0^1 x^m (1-x)^n \, dx = \left[\frac{x^{m+1}}{m+1} (1-x)^n \right]_0^1 + \int_0^1 \frac{x^{m+1}}{m+1} n (1-x)^{n-1} \, dx$$

$$= \frac{n}{m+1} \int_0^1 x^{m+1} (1-x)^{n-1} \, dx,$$

whence by successive applications of the formula we find ultimately if n be an integer that

$$\int_0^1 x^m (1-x)^n \, dx = \frac{n! \, m!}{n+m!} \int_0^1 x^{m+n} \, dx = \frac{n! \, m!}{n+m+1!}.$$

Many other important integrals can be dealt with in a similar way.

IV. INTEGRATION BY THE USE OF PARTIAL FRACTIONS

10. Any expression of the form $\frac{F(x)}{f(x)}$, where $F(x)$ and $f(x)$ are both rational integral algebraic functions of x, can be expressed as the sum of a number of terms of which the general forms are $a_r x^r$ and $\frac{b_r}{(x-c_r)^r}$. For if the degree of $F(x)$ is equal to or greater than that of $f(x)$, by division we can obtain a quotient, together with a new fraction in which the numerator is of lower degree than the denominator. The quotient provides the terms of the first form and the new fraction can be split up by partial fractions into terms of the second form. The integrals of these general forms are known and consequently the whole expression can be integrated.

The following are examples:

(1) $\quad \int \frac{(p+qx)\,dx}{(x-a)(x-b)} = \frac{1}{a-b} \int \left[\frac{aq+p}{x-a} - \frac{bq+p}{x-b} \right] dx$

$$= \frac{1}{a-b} [(aq+p) \log(x-a) - (bq+p) \log(x-b)] + c.$$

(2) $\quad \int \frac{dx}{ax^2 + 2bx + c} = \frac{1}{a} \int \frac{dx}{\left(x + \dfrac{b}{a}\right)^2 + \dfrac{ac - b^2}{a^2}}.$

The form of the integral depends upon whether $ac - b^2$ is positive or negative.

In the former case the integral clearly is equal to

$$\frac{1}{\sqrt{ac - b^2}} \tan^{-1} \frac{ax + b}{\sqrt{ac - b^2}}.$$

In the latter case the integral becomes

$$\frac{1}{2\sqrt{b^2 - ac}} \log \frac{ax + b - \sqrt{b^2 - ac}}{ax + b + \sqrt{b^2 - ac}}.$$

(3) $$\int_0^1 \frac{x^3 dx}{(x+1)(x+2)} = \int_0^1 \left[x - 3 - \frac{1}{x+1} + \frac{8}{x+2} \right] dx$$

$$= \left[\frac{x^2}{2} - 3x - \log(x+1) + 8\log(x+2) \right]_0^1$$

$$= 8\log 3 - 9\log 2 - \tfrac{5}{2}.$$

CHAPTER XIX

INTEGRAL CALCULUS. DEFINITE INTEGRALS. MISCELLANEOUS APPLICATIONS

GENERAL PROPOSITIONS

1. It is desirable to place on record several general propositions, in regard to change of limits, which are in the nature of being self-evident.

In Chapter XVI it has been shown that

$$\int_a^b f(x)\, dx = F(b) - F(a),$$

where $f(x)$ is the differential coefficient of $F(x)$.

It follows that

I. $$\int_a^b f(x)\, dx = \int_a^b f(z)\, dz \quad \dots\dots\dots\dots\dots(1),$$

since neither x nor z occurs in the result.

II. $$\int_a^b f(x)\, dx = -\int_b^a f(x)\, dx \quad \dots\dots\dots\dots\dots(2).$$

Thus the interchange of the limits results in a change of sign of the definite integral.

On the left-hand side we have regarded the increment of dx as positive, so that, while x increases from a to b, the value of the integral is $F(b) - F(a)$.

On the right-hand side the increment dx is negative and x decreases from b to a, giving a value for the integral of

$$F(a) - F(b).$$

III. $$\int_a^c f(x)\, dx = \int_b^c f(x)\, dx + \int_a^b f(x)\, dx \quad \dots\dots\dots(3).$$

For the left-hand side is $F(c) - F(a)$ and the right-hand side is $F(c) - F(b) + F(b) - F(a)$.

IV. $$\int_0^a f(x)\, dx = \int_0^a f(a - x)\, dx \quad \dots\dots\dots\dots(4).$$

For if we substitute $a - z$ for x, then when $x = a$, $z = 0$, and when $x = 0$, $z = a$.

Also $- dz = dx.$

Therefore

$$\int_0^a f(x)\, dx = \int_a^0 -f(a-z)\, dz = \int_0^a f(a-z)\, dz \quad \text{(by II)}$$

$$= \int_0^a f(a-x)\, dx \quad \text{(by I)}.$$

2. *Differentiation of Definite Integrals.*

Let $$u = \int_a^b f(x, c)\, dx$$

be a definite integral where the quantity c is independent of x, and the limits a and b are independent of c.

To find $\dfrac{du}{dc}$ let Δu be the change in u corresponding to a change Δc in c. Then, since the limits are unaltered,

$$\Delta u = \int_a^b \{f(x, c + \Delta c) - f(x, c)\}\, dx.$$

Therefore $$\frac{\Delta u}{\Delta c} = \int_a^b \frac{\{f(x, c + \Delta c) - f(x, c)\}}{\Delta c}\, dx.$$

Proceeding to the limit, we have

$$\frac{du}{dc} = \int_a^b \frac{df(x, c)}{dc}\, dx *\quad \dotfill (5).$$

Thus the differential of the definite integral is reached by a process of *differentiating under the sign of integration.*

3. An important use of this theorem is that of finding the values of other integrals from those of known form.

For example, if the equation

$$\int_0^\infty e^{-ax}\, dx = \frac{1}{a}$$

---

* The student is referred to more advanced treatises for exceptions to this general result.

be differentiated n times with respect to a, we get

$$\int_0^\infty x^n\, e^{-ax}\, dx = \frac{n!}{a^{n+1}}.$$

4. *Areas of Curves.*

It has been shown that geometrically the definite integral $\int_a^b f(x)\, dx$ represents the area enclosed between the curve $y = f(x)$ and the axis of x bounded by the ordinates $x = a$ and $x = b$.

Example 1. Prove that the area of the parabola $y^2 = 4ax$ bounded by the curve, the axis of x and any ordinate is two-thirds of the rectangle contained by the ordinate and the intercept on the axis of x.

Let $ON = b$.

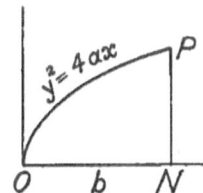

Then area $OPN = \int_0^b y\, dx = \int_0^b \sqrt{4ax}\, dx = 2a^{\frac{1}{2}}\left[\frac{2}{3} x^{\frac{3}{2}}\right]_0^b$

$$= \tfrac{4}{3} a^{\frac{1}{2}} b^{\frac{3}{2}}$$

$$= \tfrac{2}{3}(2a^{\frac{1}{2}} b^{\frac{1}{2}})\, b$$

$$= \tfrac{2}{3} PN \cdot ON$$

$$= \tfrac{2}{3} \text{ rectangle.}$$

5. *Mean Value and Probability.*

Definite Integrals can be used to find the mean value of a function whose value is changing continuously by indefinitely small increments.

Thus to find the mean value of $f(x)$ for all values of x from a to b. If we divide $b - a$ into n portions each equal to h, the mean value of the functions $f(a), f(a + h), \ldots f(a + \overline{n - 1}h)$ is

$$\frac{f(a) + f(a + h) + \ldots + f(a + \overline{n - 1}h)}{n}$$

$$= \frac{h\,[\,f(a) + f(a + h) + \ldots + f(a + \overline{n - 1}h)\,]}{b - a}$$

since $nh = b - a$.

If now we make h indefinitely small, we shall have the mean value of all values of $f(x)$ from $f(a)$ to $f(b)$. Consequently the mean value is $\dfrac{1}{b - a} \int_a^b f(x)\, dx.$

Example 2. A number n is divided at random into two parts; find the mean value of their product.

Let x be one part, then the product is $x\,(n-x)$. We have to find the mean value of this product for all values of x from 0 to n. Thus we get for the mean value

$$\frac{1}{n}\int_0^n x\,(n-x)\,dx = \frac{1}{n}\left(\frac{n^3}{2} - \frac{n^3}{3}\right) = \frac{n^2}{6}.$$

6. The class of problem in Probability that admits of being treated by the methods of the Integral Calculus can best be illustrated by an example.

Example 3. Three events A, B, C are known to have happened in the same century. What is the chance that the events happened in the order A, B, C; B happening within n years of the middle of the century?

The chance that the events happened in the order A, B, C is clearly $\frac{1}{6}$, if there is no limitation as to when B can happen, since there are six possible orders in which the events A, B, C can happen.

To ascertain the further chance that, with the events occurring in that order, B happened within n years of the middle of the century, let x be the number of years from the beginning of the century to the event B, so that B occurs during the interval of time between x and $x+dx$. Then the A cases may have occurred in any of these x years, and the C cases may have occurred in any of the following $100-x$ years. The total number of possible cases is therefore $x\,(100-x)$ in respect of the above interval of time dx.

But B must have occurred within n years of the middle of the century, therefore x can have any value between $50-n$ and $50+n$. Hence the required chance, being equal to the number of favourable cases divided by the whole number, is

$$\frac{\displaystyle\int_{50-n}^{50+n} x\,(100-x)\,dx}{\displaystyle\int_{0}^{100} x\,(100-x)\,dx} = 3\left(\frac{n}{100}\right) - 4\left(\frac{n}{100}\right)^3,$$

and the answer to the question is

$$\frac{1}{6}\left[3\left(\frac{n}{100}\right) - 4\left(\frac{n}{100}\right)^3\right] = \frac{1}{2}\left(\frac{n}{100}\right) - \frac{2}{3}\left(\frac{n}{100}\right)^3.$$

7. An example of a somewhat different type is given in the following problem.

Example 4. An event has always happened on an average once a year. Find the chance that it did not happen in a given year and prove it equals e^{-1}.

The event has happened on an average once a year. The chance that it occurred in any given nth part of a year is, therefore, $\frac{1}{n}$, and the chance that it did not occur in that period is $1 - \frac{1}{n}$.

By the ordinary rules of probability, the chance that it failed to occur in n consecutive periods each of $\frac{1}{n}$th part of a year is $\left(1 - \frac{1}{n}\right)^n$. To obtain the solution to the problem, we proceed to the limit, thus obtaining $\underset{n \to \infty}{\text{Lt}} \left(1 - \frac{1}{n}\right)^n$, which by algebra equals e^{-1}.

CHAPTER XX

APPROXIMATE INTEGRATION

1. In many cases integration, or continuous summation of the values of a function, cannot be accomplished, either because the quantity to be integrated cannot be expressed as a mathematical function, or because the function itself is not capable of being integrated directly.

In these cases formulas of approximation can be used, which may conveniently be divided into two classes, viz. formulas expressing the value of the definite integral in terms of

(i) the sum of the successive values of the function and of its derivatives,

or (ii) the values of isolated values of the function, not necessarily successive.

We shall now proceed to consider formulas of the first of these classes.

2. *The Euler-Maclaurin Expansion.*

Let
$$\Sigma f(x) = F(x),$$
so that
$$f(x) = \Delta F(x).$$

Then
$$\overset{n-1}{\underset{0}{\Sigma}}\, f(x) = f(0) + f(1) + \ldots + f(n-1)$$
$$= F(n) - F(0). \quad \text{[See Chapter VII, §4]}$$

Now
$$F(x) = \Delta^{-1} f(x)$$
$$= (e^D - 1)^{-1} f(x), \quad \text{since} \quad \Delta = e^D - 1,$$

which, by actual division,

$$= \left(\frac{1}{D} - \frac{1}{2} + \frac{D}{12} - \frac{D^3}{720} + \ldots\right) f(x)$$

$$= D^{-1} f(x) - \frac{1}{2} f(x) + \frac{1}{12}\frac{df(x)}{dx} - \frac{1}{720}\frac{d^3 f(x)}{dx^3} + \ldots$$

$$= \int f(x)\, dx - \tfrac{1}{2} f(x) + \tfrac{1}{12} f'(x) - \tfrac{1}{720} f'''(x) + \ldots.$$

Therefore
$$F(n) - F(0) = \int_0^n f(x)\, dx - \tfrac{1}{2}\{f(n) - f(0)\} + \tfrac{1}{12}\{f'(n) - f'(0)\}$$
$$- \tfrac{1}{720}\{f'''(n) - f'''(0)\} + \ldots.$$

But
$$F(n) - F(0) = f(0) + f(1) + \ldots + f(n-1).$$

Hence

$$\int_0^n f(x)\,dx = \tfrac{1}{2}f(0)+f(1)+\ldots+f(n-1)+\tfrac{1}{2}f(n)-\tfrac{1}{12}\{f'(n)-f'(0)\}$$
$$+\tfrac{1}{720}\{f'''(n)-f'''(0)\}-\ldots \qquad (1).$$

This result is not limited to the case where the ordinates are at unit distance apart, for, as has been remarked in connection with Finite Differences, by changing the origin and unit of measurement the formula can be given a more general form. Thus

$$\frac{1}{r}\int_a^{a+nr} f(x)\,dx = \tfrac{1}{2}f(a)+f(a+r)+\ldots+f(a+\overline{n-1}r)+\tfrac{1}{2}f(a+nr)$$
$$-\tfrac{1}{12}r\{f'(a+nr)-f'(a)\}+\frac{r^3}{720}\{f'''(a+nr)-f'''(a)\}$$
$$-\frac{r^5}{30240}\{f^{(v)}(a+nr)-f^{(v)}(a)\}+\ldots \qquad \ldots\ldots\ldots\ldots(2).$$

Example. Calculate $\displaystyle\int_{20}^{25}\frac{dx}{x}$.

Taking values at unit intervals we have, remembering that

$$\frac{d\left(\frac{1}{x}\right)}{dx}=-\frac{1}{x^2} \quad\text{and}\quad \frac{d^3\left(\frac{1}{x}\right)}{dx^3}=-\frac{6}{x^4},$$

$$\int_{20}^{25}\frac{dx}{x}=\frac{1}{2}\cdot\frac{1}{20}+\frac{1}{21}+\frac{1}{22}+\frac{1}{23}+\frac{1}{24}+\frac{1}{2}\cdot\frac{1}{25}-\frac{1}{12}\left(-\frac{1}{25^2}+\frac{1}{20^2}\right)$$
$$+\frac{1}{120}\left(-\frac{1}{25^4}+\frac{1}{20^4}\right)$$

$$= \cdot025000$$
$$\cdot047619$$
$$\cdot045455$$
$$\cdot043478$$
$$\cdot041667$$
$$\cdot020000$$

$$\overline{\cdot223219}-\tfrac{1}{12}(\cdot0009)+\tfrac{1}{120}(\cdot00000369)$$
$$= \cdot223144.$$

The value of the integral is clearly equal to $\log_e\frac{25}{20}$, which to five places of decimals is $\cdot22314$.

3. *Woolhouse's Formula.*

This formula gives a relationship between the sum of consecutive ordinates and the sum of equidistant ordinates at greater intervals. It can be derived from the Euler-Maclaurin formula as follows.

Formula (1) gives

$$\int_0^n f(x)\,dx = \tfrac{1}{2}f(0) + f(1) + \dots + f(n-1) + \tfrac{1}{2}f(n) - \tfrac{1}{12}\{f'(n) - f'(0)\}$$
$$+ \tfrac{1}{720}\{f'''(n) - f'''(0)\} - \dots.$$

If the interval is $\dfrac{1}{m}$ the formula becomes

$$m\int_0^n f(x)\,dx = \tfrac{1}{2}f(0) + f\left(\frac{1}{m}\right) + f\left(\frac{2}{m}\right) + \dots$$
$$+ \tfrac{1}{2}f(n) - \frac{1}{12m}\{f'(n) - f'(0)\} + \frac{1}{720m^3}\{f'''(n) - f'''(0)\} - \dots,$$

whence from the first of the above equations

$$m\int_0^n f(x)\,dx = m\{f(0) + f(1) + \dots + f(n)\}$$

$$- \frac{m}{2}\{f(0) + f(n)\} - \frac{m}{12}\{f'(n) - f'(0)\} + \frac{m}{720}\{f'''(n) - f'''(0)\} - \dots$$

and from the second equation

$$m\int_0^n f(x)\,dx = \left\{f(0) + f\left(\frac{1}{m}\right) + \dots + f(n)\right\} - \tfrac{1}{2}\{f(0) + f(n)\}$$

$$- \frac{1}{12m}\{f'(n) - f'(0)\} + \frac{1}{720m^3}\{f'''(n) - f'''(0)\} - \dots,$$

whence, by subtraction,

$$f(0) + f\left(\frac{1}{m}\right) + \dots + f(n) = m\{f(0) + f(1) + \dots + f(n)\}$$

$$- \frac{m-1}{2}\{f(0) + f(n)\} - \frac{m^2-1}{12m}\{f'(n) - f'(0)\}$$

$$+ \frac{m^4-1}{720m^3}\{f'''(n) - f'''(0)\} - \dots \quad (3).$$

4. By putting $a = 0$ and $r = 1$ in formula (2) and proceeding as above, we obtain the following result:

$$f(0) + f(1) + f(2) + \dots + f(mn) = n\{f(0) + f(n) + f(2n) + \dots$$

$$+ f(mn)\} - \frac{n-1}{2}\{f(0) + f(mn)\} - \frac{n^2-1}{12}\{f'(mn) - f'(0)\}$$

$$+ \frac{n^4-1}{720}\{f'''(mn) - f'''(0)\} - \dots \quad \quad \dots\dots(4).$$

This formula enables the sum of consecutive terms of a series to be expressed in terms of those at greater intervals. Thus the work may often be shortened, particularly where the values of individual terms of the series require to be obtained by calculation in the first instance.

5. *Lubbock's Formula.*

Lubbock's formula is similar to that of Woolhouse, but it substitutes finite differences for the differential coefficients.

Now $\qquad D = \Delta - \tfrac{1}{2}\Delta^2 + \tfrac{1}{3}\Delta^3 - \tfrac{1}{4}\Delta^4 + \ldots$

and $\qquad D^3 = \Delta^3 - \tfrac{3}{2}\Delta^4 + \ldots .$

Therefore, substituting in the above formula (3), we get

$$f(0) + f\left(\frac{1}{m}\right) + f\left(\frac{2}{m}\right) + \ldots + f(n)$$

$$= m\left\{f(0) + f(1) + f(2) + \ldots + f(n)\right\} - \frac{m-1}{2}\left\{f(0) + f(n)\right\}$$

$$- \frac{m^2 - 1}{12m}\left\{\Delta f(n) - \Delta f(0)\right\} + \frac{m^2 - 1}{24m}\left\{\Delta^2 f(n) - \Delta^2 f(0)\right\}$$

$$- \frac{(m^2 - 1)(19m^2 - 1)}{720m^3}\left\{\Delta^3 f(n) - \Delta^3 f(0)\right\}$$

$$+ \frac{(m^2 - 1)(9m^2 - 1)}{480m^3}\left\{\Delta^4 f(n) - \Delta^4 f(0)\right\} + \ldots \qquad (5).$$

6.

By an alteration in the unit of measurement the formula may be expressed as

$$f(0) + f(1) + f(2) + \ldots + f(mn) = n\left\{f(0) + f(n) + f(2n) + \ldots + f(mn)\right\}$$

$$- \frac{n-1}{2}\left\{f(0) + f(mn)\right\} - \frac{n^2 - 1}{12n}\left\{\Delta f(mn) - \Delta f(0)\right\}$$

$$+ \frac{n^2 - 1}{24n}\left\{\Delta^2 f(mn) - \Delta^2 f(0)\right\}$$

$$- \frac{(n^2 - 1)(19n^2 - 1)}{720n^3}\left\{\Delta^3 f(mn) - \Delta^3 f(0)\right\}$$

$$+ \frac{(n^2 - 1)(9n^2 - 1)}{480n^3}\left\{\Delta^4 f(mn) - \Delta^4 f(0)\right\} + \ldots \qquad (6),$$

where Δ, Δ^2, ... express the values of the differences taken over the interval n, and not those taken over unit intervals.

In this form the formula corresponds to formula (4) given above.

7. In cases where the terms of a series decrease steadily and the term corresponding to the upper limit tends to the value zero, the above formulas can be simplified somewhat, since the final term of the series, its differences and derived functions all vanish. Also it is frequently the case that the end terms of the series are unimportant and thus m and n may be taken at any suitable figures so as to correspond with tabulated values of the function.

To illustrate this we will calculate, first by Woolhouse's formula and then by Lubbock's, the value of $\displaystyle\sum_{x=10}^{x=\infty} (1\cdot1)^{-x}$.

Example 1. By Woolhouse's formula.

Let us use formula (4) and take $n = 15$. The values of $(1\cdot1)^{-x}$ tend to become unimportant when $x = 100$, therefore we will take $m = 6$ and ignore the values of the differential coefficients at the upper limit.

Then

$$f(x) = (1\cdot1)^{-x}, \quad f'(x) = -(1\cdot1)^x \log_e 1\cdot1, \quad f'''(x) = -(1\cdot1)^x (\log_e 1\cdot1)^3.$$

Also $\qquad\qquad\qquad \log_e 1\cdot1 = \cdot09531.$

Thus we get

x	$(1\cdot1)^{-x}$	
10	$\cdot38554$	$\dfrac{15-1}{2}(1\cdot1)^{-10} = 2\cdot6988$
25	$\cdot09230$	
40	$\cdot02209$	$\dfrac{15^2-1}{12}\times(1\cdot1)^{-10}\times\cdot09531 = \cdot6859$
55	$\cdot00529$	
70	$\cdot00127$	$\dfrac{15^4-1}{720}\times(1\cdot1)^{-10}\times(\cdot09531)^3 = \cdot0234$
85	$\cdot00030$	
100	$\cdot00007$	
	$\overline{\cdot50686}\times15 = 7\cdot6029$	

And the final result is

$$7\cdot6029 - 2\cdot6988 - \cdot6859 + \cdot0234 = 4\cdot2416.$$

The true value is, of course,

$$\frac{(1\cdot1)^{-10}}{1 - \dfrac{1}{1\cdot1}} = 4\cdot2410,$$

which shows that the error involved by disregarding the final terms of the series is small.

Example 2. By Lubbock's formula.

In this example we will take $n = 10$, using formula (6).

x	$(1 \cdot 1)^{-x}$	Δ	Δ^2	Δ^3	Δ^4
10	·38554	− ·23690	+ ·14557	− ·08946	+ ·05500
20	·14864	·09133	·05611	·03446	
30	·05731	·03522	·02165		
40	·02209	·01357			
50	·00852				
60	·00328				
70	·00127				
80	·00049				
90	·00019				
100	·00007				

$$-\frac{9}{2} f(10) = -1\cdot7349$$

$$\frac{99}{120}\Delta = -\cdot1954$$

$$-\frac{99}{240}\Delta^2 = -\cdot0600$$

$$\frac{99 \times 1899}{720,000}\Delta^3 = -\cdot0233$$

$$-\frac{99 \times 899}{480,000}\Delta^4 = -\cdot0102$$

$$-\overline{2\cdot0238}$$

$\cdot62740 \times 10 = 6\cdot2740$

The result is $6\cdot2740 - 2\cdot0238 = 4\cdot2502$ as compared with the true value of $4\cdot2410$.

8. The above examples illustrate points of disadvantage which may arise in connection with the formulas.

Woolhouse's formula can only be applied to a mathematical function where the differential coefficients can be obtained. In other cases, Lubbock's formula must be used, and then it may often happen that the terms in the formula do not converge sufficiently rapidly to give a good result, unless a large number of terms is used. This accounts for the relatively poor result shown in the example above. If intervals of 15 had been used instead of 10, a worse result would have been shown.

Some of these disadvantages can be met by the use of the formulas given in the following Articles.

OTHER FORMULAS OF APPROXIMATE INTEGRATION

9. The definite integral of any function can be expressed in terms of the individual values of any number of ordinates by assuming that the function can be represented, to a sufficient degree of approximation, by a parabolic function of the requisite degree in x.

10. Thus to express the value of $\int_{0}^{2} f(x)\,dx$ in terms of $f(0)$, $f(1)$ and $f(2)$, let $f(x) = a + bx + cx^2$.

[N.B. Since we are to express the result in terms of *three* values of the function, we introduce *three* terms involving *three* unknown constants a, b and c in the expression representing $f(x)$.]

Then

$$\int_0^2 f(x)\,dx = \int_0^2 (a + bx + cx^2)\,dx$$

$$= \left[ax + \frac{bx^2}{2} + \frac{cx^3}{3} \right]_0^2$$

$$= 2a + 2b + \frac{8c}{3}.$$

Also

$$f(0) = a,$$
$$f(1) = a + b + c,$$
$$f(2) = a + 2b + 4c.$$

These equations could be solved for a, b and c, and the resulting values substituted in the value of the integral found above.

Alternatively, we may proceed as follows:

Let

$$\int_0^2 f(x)\,dx = pf(0) + qf(1) + rf(2).$$

Then

$$2a + 2b + \frac{8c}{3} = pa + q(a + b + c) + r(a + 2b + 4c),$$

so that

$$p + q + r = 2,$$
$$q + 2r = 2,$$
$$q + 4r = \tfrac{8}{3}.$$

Whence

$$r = \tfrac{1}{3}, \quad q = \tfrac{4}{3}, \quad p = \tfrac{1}{3},$$

and

$$\int_0^2 f(x)\,dx = \frac{f(0) + 4f(1) + f(2)}{3} \quad \ldots\ldots\ldots\ldots(7).$$

By analogy we may write

$$\int_0^{2n} f(x)\,dx = \frac{n}{3}\{f(0) + 4f(n) + f(2n)\} \quad \ldots\ldots\ldots(8).$$

This result is known as *Simpson's Rule*.

By dividing the whole area from 0 to $2n$ into n consecutive equal spaces and applying Simpson's rule to each, we obtain

$$\int_0^{2n} f(x)\,dx = \frac{1}{3}\{f(0) + 4f(1) + 2f(2) + 4f(3) + 2f(4) + \ldots$$
$$+ f(2n)\}\ldots(9).$$

This formula should normally yield better results than a single application of the formula (8) over the whole range of integration. It can, of course, only be applied where a sufficient number of values of the function to be integrated is available.

11. Where the number of terms is four, by proceeding in a similar manner to the above, we arrive at the result

$$\int_0^{3n} f(x)\, dx = \frac{3n}{8} \{f(0) + 3f(1) + 3f(2) + f(3)\} \quad \ldots(10).$$

12. The process of obtaining the desired formula may be simplified somewhat, when the given terms are arranged symmetrically about the central point, by adopting the central point as origin.

This may be illustrated by proving the well-known *Weddle's Rule*.

In this case $\int_0^6 f(x)\, dx$ is to be expressed in terms of

$$f(0),\ f(1),\ \ldots f(6).$$

Let $\qquad f(x) = a + bx + cx^2 + dx^3 + ex^4 + fx^5 + gx^6.$

Then $\qquad \int_{-3}^{+3} f(x)\, dx = 6a + 18c + \frac{486}{5} e + \frac{4374}{7} g.$

Also $\qquad\qquad f(0) = a,$

$$f(1) + f(-1) = 2a + 2c + 2e + 2g,$$
$$f(2) + f(-2) = 2a + 8c + 32e + 128g,$$
$$f(3) + f(-3) = 2a + 18c + 162e + 1458g.$$

Solving these equations for a, c, e and g, and substituting the resulting values of these constants in the expression for the integral, we obtain

$$\int_{-3}^{+3} f(x)\, dx = \frac{1}{140} \{272f(0) + 27\overline{f(1) + f(-1)}$$
$$+ 216\overline{f(2) + f(-2)} + 41\overline{f(3) + f(-3)}\}.$$

This is not in a very convenient form for numerical work, so we add

$$\frac{1}{140} \Delta^6 f(-3) = \frac{1}{140} \{-20f(0) + 15\overline{f(1) + f(-1)}$$
$$- 6\overline{f(2) + f(-2)} + \overline{f(3) + f(-3)}\},$$

thus giving

$$\int_{-3}^{+3} f(x)\,dx + \frac{1}{140}\,\Delta^6 f(-3) = \frac{1}{140}\,\{252f(0) + 42\overline{f(1) + f(-1)}$$
$$+ 210\overline{f(2) + f(-2)} + 42\overline{f(3) + f(-3)}\}.$$

Neglecting the term $\frac{1}{140}\,\Delta^6 f(-3)$ which will usually be very small, we arrive at the final result

$$\int_{-3}^{+3} f(x)\,dx = \frac{3}{10}\,\{f(3) + 5f(2) + f(1) + 6f(0) + f(-1)$$
$$+ 5f(-2) + f(-3)\}\ldots(11),$$

or, changing the origin,

$$\int_{0}^{6} f(x)\,dx = \frac{3}{10}\,\{f(0) + 5f(1) + f(2) + 6f(3) + f(4)$$
$$+ 5f(5) + f(6)\}\ldots(12).$$

13. Another powerful formula can be obtained by expressing $\int_{0}^{6} f(x)\,dx$ in terms of $f(0)$, $f(1)$, $f(3)$, $f(5)$ and $f(6)$.

Having five values of the function, let

$$f(x) = a + bx + cx^2 + dx^3 + ex^4.$$

Then
$$\int_{-3}^{+3} f(x)\,dx = 6a + 18c + \frac{486}{5}\,e.$$

Also
$$f(0) = a,$$
$$f(2) + f(-2) = 2a + 8c + 32e,$$
$$f(3) + f(-3) = 2a + 18c + 162e.$$

Solving for a, c and e, and substituting in the equation for the integral, we find

$$\int_{-3}^{+3} f(x)\,dx = 2\cdot2\,f(0) + 1\cdot62\,\{f(2) + f(-2)\} + \cdot28\,\{f(3) + f(-3)\},$$

or, altering the origin and limits,

$$\int_{0}^{6n} f(x)\,dx = n\,\{\cdot28\overline{f(0) + f(6n)} + 1\cdot62\overline{f(n) + f(5n)} + 2\cdot2f(3n)\}$$
$$\ldots\ldots\ldots(13).$$

Similarly

$$\int_{6n}^{12n} f(x)\,dx = n\,\{\cdot28\overline{f(6n) + f(12n)} + 1\cdot62\overline{f(7n) + f(11n)}$$
$$+ 2\cdot2\,f(9n)\}.$$

Then $\displaystyle\int_0^\infty f(x)\,dx = \int_0^{6n} f(x)\,dx + \int_{6n}^{12n} f(x)\,dx + \dots$

$$= n\,[\cdot 28\,\{f(0)+2f(6n)+2f(12n)+\dots\}$$
$$+1\cdot 62\,\{f(n)+f(5n)+f(7n)+\dots\}$$
$$+2\cdot 2\,\{f(3n)+f(9n)+\dots\}].$$

Now in a series of values decreasing to zero, if $7n$ be so chosen as to fall just within or just without the limits of the table of the function to be integrated, we obtain the convenient formula

$$\int_0^\infty f(x)\,dx = n\,\{\cdot 28\,f(0)+1\cdot 62 f(n)+2\cdot 2 f(3n)+1\cdot 62 f(5n)$$
$$+\cdot 56\,f(6n)+1\cdot 62\,f(7n)\}\dots(14).$$

The formulas in this Article are due to G. F. Hardy and the last is usually known among actuaries as $39\,(a)$, since that is the number assigned to it in the original Text Book, Part II.

14. A useful formula, involving only a simple summation of certain terms of the given series, is as follows:

$$\int_0^{10n} f(x)\,dx = \frac{10n}{4}\,[f(n)+f(4n)+f(6n)+f(9n)]\dots(15).$$

By expanding $f(x)$ in a series of ascending powers of x by Maclaurin's Theorem, it is easy to show that the formula involves a small second difference error. It can, however, be used conveniently where only a rough result is required.

15. An alternative method of obtaining formulas of this character is to express $f(x)$ in terms of the given values of the function. This can be done by Lagrange's formula and the resulting expression is then integrated between the desired limits.

As an example, we will develop formula (13) in this way.

The given values of the function are $f(3), f(2), f(0), f(-2)$ and $f(-3)$. Then

$$f(x) = \frac{(x+2)\,x\,(x-2)\,(x-3)}{-1\times -3\times -5\times -6}f(-3) + \frac{(x+3)\,x\,(x-2)\,(x-3)}{1\times -2\times -4\times -5}f(-2)$$
$$+\frac{(x+3)\,(x+2)\,(x-2)\,(x-3)}{3\times 2\times -2\times -3}f(0) + \frac{(x+3)\,(x+2)\,x\,(x-3)}{5\times 4\times 2\times -1}f(2)$$
$$+\frac{(x+3)\,(x+2)\,x\,(x-2)}{6\times 5\times 3\times 1}f(3).$$

Therefore

$$\int_{-3}^{+3} f(x)\, dx = f(-3)\int_{-3}^{+3} \frac{(x+2)\, x\, (x-2)\, (x-3)}{90}\, dx + \text{similar terms}$$

$$= \cdot 28 f(-3) + 1 \cdot 62 f(-2) + 2 \cdot 2 f(0) + 1 \cdot 62 f(2) + \cdot 28 f(3)$$

as before.

16. The above methods are perfectly general and afford means of expressing the value of an integral in terms of any given values of the function.

It will be of value to indicate the method of application and to show the degree of accuracy in each case by applying them to an example.

Thus $$\int_{2}^{8} \frac{dx}{x} = 2 \log_e 2 = 1 \cdot 38630.$$

(i) Simpson's rule applied once gives

$$\tfrac{3}{8}(\tfrac{1}{2} + \tfrac{4}{5} + \tfrac{1}{8}) = 1 \cdot 42500.$$

(ii) Simpson's rule applied three times over the values 2–4, 4–6, 6–8 gives

$$\tfrac{1}{3}(\tfrac{1}{2} + \tfrac{4}{3} + \tfrac{2}{4} + \tfrac{4}{5} + \tfrac{2}{6} + \tfrac{4}{7} + \tfrac{1}{8}) = 1 \cdot 38770.$$

(iii) The "three-eighths" rule gives

$$\tfrac{6}{8}(\tfrac{1}{2} + \tfrac{3}{4} + \tfrac{3}{6} + \tfrac{1}{8}) = 1 \cdot 40625.$$

(iv) Weddle's rule gives

$$\tfrac{3}{10}(\tfrac{1}{2} + \tfrac{5}{3} + \tfrac{1}{4} + \tfrac{6}{5} + \tfrac{1}{6} + \tfrac{5}{7} + \tfrac{1}{8}) = 1 \cdot 38679.$$

(v) Formula (13) gives

$$\left\{ \cdot 28\,(\tfrac{1}{2} + \tfrac{1}{8}) + 1 \cdot 62\,(\tfrac{1}{3} + \tfrac{1}{7}) + \frac{2 \cdot 2}{5} \right\} = 1 \cdot 38643.$$

(vi) If formula (15) is used, $n = \cdot 6$ and we get

$$\frac{6}{4}\left[\frac{1}{2 \cdot 6} + \frac{1}{4 \cdot 4} + \frac{1}{5 \cdot 6} + \frac{1}{7 \cdot 4} \right] = 1 \cdot 38839.$$

As the values of the function are changing rapidly over the period used, the above is a somewhat severe test of the formulas. It will be noticed, however, that Weddle's rule and formula (13) differ from the true value only in the fourth place of decimals.

CHAPTER XXI

PROBABILITY

1. In considering the subject of Probability a clear appreciation must be obtained of the distinction between its mathematical or theoretical treatment and its arithmetical or practical development which is the basis of actuarial science. The difference between these two points of view will become clear by examining a few simple illustrations.

Probability or chance is merely an expression of relative degrees of uncertainty in relation to an event in respect of which our knowledge is incomplete. In the ordinary phenomena of life probabilities may not have a numerical value although distinctions are drawn. Thus we should say, in the absence of more precise knowledge, that a man of 30 was as likely as not to die before another man of 30, would most probably outlive a man of 60 and would almost certainly outlive a man of 80. The mind has clearly formed definite opinions on these points but the respective probabilities cannot be expressed in numerical form without further analysis.

2. To obtain a measure of probability some unit must be taken, and for reasons of convenience it has been the universal custom to take absolute certainty as having unit probability. Starting from this standard, certain probabilities can be found from general reasoning, whereas others, such as the chance of dying in a year, or of becoming the father of twins, must be deduced from the observation of suitable statistics.

3. As an example of the former class, one may say that, on tossing a coin, it is certain that either "heads" or "tails" will appear, and as these possibilities are equally likely, the chance that heads will appear is clearly $\frac{1}{2}$.

We cannot however assume from this that, if we toss a coin four times, two heads and two tails will necessarily appear. Indeed, as will be shown later, the respective probabilities are

$$
\begin{array}{lll}
\text{0 heads 4 tails} & \tfrac{1}{16} \\
\text{1 head \ 3 tails} & \tfrac{1}{4} \\
\text{2 heads 2 tails} & \tfrac{3}{8} \\
\text{3 heads 1 tail} & \tfrac{1}{4} \\
\text{4 heads 0 tails} & \tfrac{1}{16} \\
\hline
& \underline{1}
\end{array}
$$

What we understand is that, if the number of trials were sufficiently extended, the proportion of cases in which heads appeared would approximate more and more closely to $\tfrac{1}{2}$. It is in this sense that the mathematical definition of probability is to be understood in connection with actuarial work.

The following Articles deal with the treatment of the subject from its mathematical aspect.

4. From the foregoing considerations it will be evident that *if an event can happen in 'a' ways and fail in 'b' ways, and each of these ways is equally likely, the probability of its happening is* $\dfrac{a}{a+b}$, *and that of its failing is* $\dfrac{b}{a+b}$. For the sum of these two probabilities gives the chance of its either happening or failing, which is necessarily unity.

Alternatively, we may say that *the probability of an event is equal to the ratio of the number of cases favourable to the event, to the total number of cases.*

It follows that if p is the probability that an event will happen, the probability of its not happening is $1-p$.

5. Another method of statement is to say that *the odds are 'a' to 'b' in favour of the event or 'b' to 'a' against the event.*

Example. The chance of throwing a four at a single throw of a die is $\tfrac{1}{6}$, for there is one favourable result (a 4) and five unfavourable results (1, 2, 3, 5 or 6), all of which are equally likely.

The chance of *not* throwing a four is $\tfrac{5}{6}$, or, in other words, the odds are 5 to 1 against the event.

6. The following proposition is also self-evident:

If an event can happen in more than one way (all ways being, however, mutually exclusive), the probability of its happening at all is the sum of the several probabilities of its happening in the several ways.

Thus if the chance of scoring a "bull" be $\frac{1}{10}$, that of scoring an "inner" be $\frac{1}{8}$, that of scoring a "magpie" be $\frac{1}{6}$, and that of scoring an "outer" be $\frac{1}{4}$, the total chance of hitting the target at all (all events being mutually exclusive) must be $\frac{1}{10} + \frac{1}{8} + \frac{1}{6} + \frac{1}{4} = \frac{27}{40}$.

7. The solution of elementary questions in probability depends therefore upon general reasoning, but calculation is aided in some cases by the theorems of permutations and combinations.

Some elementary examples will now be given:

(1) The odds in a given race against three horses are 11 to 4, 13 to 3, and 7 to 2 respectively. Find the chance that one of them will win the race, a dead-heat being assumed to be impossible.

The chance that the first   horse should win is $\frac{4}{15}$,

     „   „   second   „   „ $\frac{3}{16}$,

     „   „   third   „   „ $\frac{2}{9}$.

Thus the chance that one of them should win is

$$\frac{4}{15} + \frac{3}{16} + \frac{2}{9} = \frac{487}{720}.$$

(2) *A* has three shares in a lottery where there are three prizes and six blanks. *B* has one share in another, where there is one prize and two blanks. Show that *A* has a better chance of winning a prize than *B* in the ratio of 16 to 7.

To be successful *A* may draw either 3, 2 or 1 prizes.

He may draw 3 prizes in 1 way.

He may draw 2 prizes and 1 blank in $\binom{3}{2} \times \binom{6}{1} = 18$ ways.

He may draw 1 prize and 2 blanks in $\binom{3}{1} \times \binom{6}{2} = 45$ ways.

The total number of ways in which he can win at least one prize is therefore $1 + 18 + 45 = 64$.

Now three tickets can be selected in $\binom{9}{3} = 84$ ways.

Therefore *A*'s chance of success is $\frac{64}{84} = \frac{16}{21}$.

B's chance is clearly $\frac{1}{3}$.

Therefore *A*'s chance is to *B*'s chance in the ratio 16 : 7.

Alternatively *A* may draw all blanks in $\binom{6}{3} = 20$ ways. His chance of non-success is therefore $\frac{20}{84}$ and his chance of success $1 - \frac{20}{84} = \frac{16}{21}$ as before.

(3) If four cards be drawn from a pack, what is the chance that there will be one from each suit?

Four cards can be selected from the pack in $\binom{52}{4} = 270725$ ways.

Four cards can be selected so as to be one from each suit in $13^4 = 28561$ ways.

Therefore the required chance is $\frac{28561}{270725} = \frac{2197}{20825}$.

(4) Out of a bag containing 12 balls, 5 are drawn and replaced, and afterwards 6 are drawn. Find the chance that exactly 3 balls were common to the two drawings.

The total number of ways of making the second drawing is $\binom{12}{6} = 924$.

To comply with the conditions, it must contain 3 balls out of the first 5 chosen, and 3 balls out of the 7 left on the first choice. The respective ways of making these selections are $\binom{5}{3}$ and $\binom{7}{3}$. The total number of selections favourable to the event is therefore $\binom{5}{3} \times \binom{7}{3} = 350$, and the required chance is $\frac{350}{924} = \frac{25}{66}$.

(5) Twelve persons take their places at a round table. What is the chance of two particular persons sitting together?

Let the two persons be A and B. Then, since we are only concerned with the *relative* positions of the persons, we may regard A's place as fixed. There are then 11 other seats in all, 2 of which are adjacent to A. B's chance of occupying one of these is therefore $\frac{2}{11}$.

(6) What is the chance of throwing more than 10 in a single throw with two dice?

A score of more than 10 can be made by the following throws:

$$5 \text{ and } 6, \quad 6 \text{ and } 5, \quad 6 \text{ and } 6.$$

The total possible number of combinations is $6 \times 6 = 36$ and, as 3 of these are favourable to the event, the required chance is $\frac{3}{36} = \frac{1}{12}$.

It should be noted that exactly 11 can be thrown in two ways, since (regarding the throws as consecutive) either a 6 or a 5 may appear first, but 12 can only be thrown in one way.

8. If the chance of an event is p and the measure of the quantity dependent on the event be x, the product px is called the *expectation*.

Thus we may have the *expectation* of a person in a lottery, or the *expected value* of a prize, or the *expected number* of deaths among a given number of persons, and so on.

Examples.

(1) What is the expectation of a person who is to draw one envelope from a bag which contains one £1 note, two 10s. notes and three blank pieces of paper, each placed in an envelope of uniform size?

The chance of drawing the £1 note is $\frac{1}{6}$.

The chance of drawing a 10s. note is $\frac{1}{3}$.

The value of the expectation is therefore

$$\tfrac{1}{6} \times 20s. + \tfrac{1}{3} \times 10s. = 6s.\ 8d.$$

(2) If the chance of dying in a year is $\frac{1}{20}$, the expected number of deaths among 100 people is $\frac{1}{20} \times 100 = 5$.

9. In the foregoing articles we have considered what are, in principle, single events. We have now to determine the appropriate formulas for combinations of two or more events.

In considering problems of this kind, a close watch must be made to see if the events are dependent or independent.

Thus, a bag contains 6 white and 4 black balls, and it is desired to estimate the combined chance of drawing at the first draw 3 white balls and at the second draw 3 black balls. If the balls are replaced after the first draw, the second event is clearly independent of the first. But, if they are not replaced, the drawing of 3 white balls at the first draw will obviously affect the chance of drawing 3 black balls at the second draw, and the two events will be dependent.

Dependent events are also called *contingent*.

10. We are thus led to the following proposition:

The chance of two independent events happening is the product of the chances of their happening severally.

For if the first event can happen in a ways and fail in b ways, and the corresponding figures for the second event are a' and b', the total possible combinations of events are $(a + b)(a' + b')$. Of these

Both events may happen in aa' ways.

The first event may happen and the second event fail in ab' ways.

The first event may fail and the second event happen in ba' ways.

Both events may fail in bb' ways.

The chance of their both happening is therefore $\dfrac{aa'}{(a+b)(a'+b')}$

or $\dfrac{a}{a+b} \cdot \dfrac{a'}{a'+b'}$, i.e. the product of the respective chances of their happening.

If the respective chances are p and q,

the chance that both happen is pq,

the chance that the first happens and the second fails is $p(1-q)$,

the chance that the first fails and the second happens is $(1-p)q$,

the chance that both fail is $(1-p)(1-q)$,

the chance that at least one happens is $1-(1-p)(1-q)$
$$= p+q-pq,$$

the chance that one and only one happens is

$$p(1-q)+(1-p)q$$
$$= p+q-2pq.$$

11. The above results can be applied by a slight modification of reasoning to events which are not independent.

Thus if p be the chance of the event happening, and q be the chance of a second event happening *when the first has happened,* then the chance that both should happen is pq.

12. By successive applications of the above reasoning we can arrive at a formula for any number of events.

Thus if p be the probability of an event A; and, when A has happened, q be the probability of another event B; and when A and B have happened, r be the probability of another event C; and so on for any number of events; the chance that all the events will happen is the product $pqr\ldots$.

It follows that if p be the chance that an event will happen in one trial, the chance that it will happen in each of a series of r trials is p^r, and the chance that it will happen at least once in a series of r trials is $1-(1-p)^r$.

13. This result can be developed more generally in the following way:

If p be the probability of an event happening in one trial, what is the probability of its happening once, twice, three times, ... exactly in n trials?

Let q be the probability that the event does not happen, so that $p + q = 1$. Then if the event is to happen exactly r times, it must happen in each of a given combination of r of the trials and fail in each of the remaining $(n - r)$ trials. The chance of this occurring is, as seen above, $p^r q^{n-r}$. But the particular set of r trials can be chosen in $\binom{n}{r}$ ways, each of which is equally likely. Therefore the total chance of its happening exactly r times is $\binom{n}{r} p^r q^{n-r}$, or the term containing p^r in the expansion of $(p + q)^n$.

Thus the successive terms of this expansion represent the probabilities of the event occurring respectively n, $n - 1$, $n - 2$, ... times in n trials.

14. The foregoing propositions can best be grasped by applying them to certain examples.

(i) If four cards be drawn from a pack, what is the chance that there will be one from each suit?

Let one card be drawn, which may be of any suit. The chance that a second card is of a different suit is $\frac{39}{51}$, for there are 51 cards remaining, 39 of which will be of different suits from the first. Similarly the chance of drawing a third card of a different suit from the first two is $\frac{26}{50}$, and that of a fourth different card is $\frac{13}{49}$.

The combined chance is therefore $\frac{39}{51} \times \frac{26}{50} \times \frac{13}{49} = \frac{2197}{20825}$.

This result should be compared with that obtained in Example 3 of § 7, where the problem was treated as that of a simple probability. It is clear that the same result must be obtained whether the cards are treated as being drawn simultaneously or successively.

(ii) A man throws a six-faced die until he gets an ace; he is to receive £1 if he succeeds at the first throw, £$\frac{1}{2}$ if he succeeds at the second throw, £$\frac{1}{3}$ if he succeeds at the third throw, and so on; given that $\log_e 6 = 1{\cdot}79176$, find the value of his expectation.

The chance of succeeding at the first throw is $\frac{1}{6}$. The chance of succeeding at the second throw is compounded of the chance of failing at the first throw and succeeding at the second throw, etc.

The value of the expectation is therefore

$$\tfrac{1}{6} + \tfrac{5}{6} \cdot \tfrac{1}{6} \cdot \tfrac{1}{2} + (\tfrac{5}{6})^2 \cdot \tfrac{1}{6} \cdot \tfrac{1}{3} + \dots$$
$$= \tfrac{1}{5} \{\tfrac{5}{6} + (\tfrac{5}{6})^2 \cdot \tfrac{1}{2} + (\tfrac{5}{6})^3 \cdot \tfrac{1}{3} + \dots\}$$
$$= \tfrac{1}{5} \{- \log_e (1 - \tfrac{5}{6})\}$$
$$= \tfrac{1}{5} \log_e 6$$
$$= \cdot 3583 = 7s.\ 2d.$$

(iii) Let it be assumed that the probabilities of dying within ten years after the ages specified are, on the average, as follows:

Age	Probability of dying within next 10 years
30	$\tfrac{1}{12}$
40	$\tfrac{1}{9}$
50	$\tfrac{1}{5}$

What is the chance

(a) that a person A now aged 30 should die between the ages of 50 and 60 ;

(b) that two persons A and B, aged respectively 30 and 40, should be alive 10 years hence ;

(c) that of two persons A and B, aged respectively 30 and 40, A should die between the ages of 40 and 50 and B should survive to the age of 60 ?

(a) The required chance is compounded of the chances that A should survive successively to ages 40 and 50 and should then die within the next ten years.

The several chances are $(1 - \tfrac{1}{12})$, $(1 - \tfrac{1}{9})$ and $\tfrac{1}{5}$; and the required chance is the product of these three factors, namely

$$\tfrac{11}{12} \times \tfrac{8}{9} \times \tfrac{1}{5} = \tfrac{22}{135}.$$

(b) The respective chances of surviving ten years are $(1 - \tfrac{1}{12})$ and $(1 - \tfrac{1}{9})$. The chance that both A and B should survive that period is therefore

$$\tfrac{11}{12} \times \tfrac{8}{9} = \tfrac{22}{27}.$$

(c) The chance that A should die between the ages of 40 and 50 is $\tfrac{11}{12} \times \tfrac{1}{9}$.

The chance that B should survive to the age of 60 is $\tfrac{8}{9} \times \tfrac{4}{5}$.

The required chance that these two events should both happen is, therefore,

$$(\tfrac{11}{12} \times \tfrac{1}{9}) \times (\tfrac{8}{9} \times \tfrac{4}{5}) = \tfrac{88}{1215}.$$

(iv) The faces of a die are marked with the consecutive numbers 1, 2, ... 6. What is the chance that, after seven throws, the sum of the numbers exhibited equals 30 exactly ?

This example is important, as it illustrates a method which can frequently be employed.

The number of ways in which the seven numbers exhibited can total 30 is given by the coefficient of x^{30} in the expansion of

$$(x + x^2 + \ldots + x^6)^7,$$

for this coefficient arises from the combination of the indices of x, taken together in such a way as to produce a total of 30.

Writing $(x + x^2 + \ldots + x^6)^7$ as $x^7 (1 - x^6)^7 (1 - x)^{-7}$ it is seen that we require the coefficient of x^{23} in the expansion of

$$(1 - x^6)^7 (1 - x)^{-7} = (1 - 7x^6 + 21x^{12} - 35x^{18} + \ldots)(1 - x)^{-7}.$$

The expression within the first bracket need not be expanded further, since no term higher than x^{23} is required. It remains to combine the given terms with appropriate terms taken from the expansion of the second bracket in such a way that the power of x given by the product of the two terms is 23.

Thus we get

$$(1) \times \left(\frac{24 \times \ldots \times 29}{1 \times \ldots \times 6} x^{23} \right) = \quad 475{,}020 \; x^{23}$$

$$(- 7x^6) \times \left(\frac{18 \times \ldots \times 23}{1 \times \ldots \times 6} x^{17} \right) = - 706{,}629 \; x^{23}$$

$$(21x^{12}) \times \left(\frac{12 \times \ldots \times 17}{1 \times \ldots \times 6} x^{11} \right) = \quad 259{,}896 \; x^{23}$$

$$(- 35x^{18}) \times \left(\frac{6 \times \ldots \times 11}{1 \times \ldots \times 6} x^5 \right) = - 16{,}170 \; x^{23}$$

$$\overline{ 12{,}117 \; x^{23}}$$

The number of ways in which a total of exactly 30 can be made is thus 12,117.

Now, on any of the seven throws, any of the six numbers may be exhibited. The total number of possible combinations of numbers is, therefore, 6^7. The number of combinations giving a total of 30 being 12,117, the required chance is $\dfrac{12{,}117}{6^7}$.

15. The following miscellaneous examples are taken from the examination papers of the Institute ; they illustrate various devices which may be employed with advantage in the solution of questions of this character.

(i) If n whole numbers be multiplied together, find the chance that the last digit of the product is a five.　[1910, Paper I, Q. 7.]

The chance is compounded of the separate chances that none of the final digits of the n numbers is even and that one at least is a five.

The required chance is therefore

$$(\tfrac{1}{2})^n \{1 - (\tfrac{4}{5})^n\} = \frac{5^n - 4^n}{10^n}.$$

(ii) Four coins are tossed together and A is to receive £2 if exactly 2 heads turn up, and to pay £1 in any other event. Find .... the probability that after four trials A is £1 out of pocket. [1913, Paper I, Q. 8.]

To satisfy the conditions A must win once and lose thrice.

The chance that exactly 2 heads turn up equals the middle term in the expansion of $(\tfrac{1}{2} + \tfrac{1}{2})^4 = \binom{4}{2} \times (\tfrac{1}{2})^4 = \tfrac{3}{8}$.

Therefore the chance that he should win once and lose thrice equals the second term in the expansion of $(\tfrac{5}{8} + \tfrac{3}{8})^4$, which is

$$4 . \tfrac{3}{8} . (\tfrac{5}{8})^3 = \tfrac{375}{1024}.$$

(iii) If a coin be tossed 15 times, what is the probability of getting heads exactly as many times in the first 10 throws as in the last 5?　[1915, Paper I, Q. 9.]

If n coins be tossed the chance that exactly r heads turn up equals the $(r + 1)$th term in the expansion of $(\tfrac{1}{2} + \tfrac{1}{2})^n$.

Now in the last 5 throws we may get $0, 1, \dots 5$ heads and we have to combine the chance of any of these with the chance of getting the same number of heads in the first 10 throws. Thus we have for the several chances of getting

0 heads in both sets of throws	=		$(\tfrac{1}{2})^5$.		$(\tfrac{1}{2})^{10}$
1 head	,,	,,	,,	$= 5(\tfrac{1}{2})^5$.	$10(\tfrac{1}{2})^{10}$
2 heads	,,	,,	,,	$= 10(\tfrac{1}{2})^5$.	$45(\tfrac{1}{2})^{10}$
3 ,,	,,	,,	,,	$= 10(\tfrac{1}{2})^5 . 120(\tfrac{1}{2})^{10}$	
4 ,,	,,	,,	,,	$= 5(\tfrac{1}{2})^5 . 210(\tfrac{1}{2})^{10}$	
5 ,,	,,	,,	,,	$= (\tfrac{1}{2})^5 . 252(\tfrac{1}{2})^{10}$	

Therefore the total chance that the same number will turn up in both sets of throws is the sum of each of these distinct probabilities, i.e. $\dfrac{3003}{2^{15}}$.

(iv) A and B throw for a certain stake, each throwing with one die; A's die is marked 2, 3, 4, 5, 6, 7, and B's 1, 2, 3, 4, 5, 6, and equal throws divide the stake; prove that A's expectation is $\frac{47}{72}$ of the stake.

What will A's expectation be if equal throws go for nothing? [1911, Paper I, Q. 8.]

Let e equal A's expectation.

The chance of A's throwing any of the numbers marked on the die is the same for each number.

If A throws a 2, B must throw a 1 if A is to win the stake, or a 2 if A is to divide the stake. The chance that A throws a 2 is $\frac{1}{6}$; the chance that he then wins the stake is $\frac{1}{6}$ and that he divides the stake is also $\frac{1}{6}$. His expectation if he throws a 2 is therefore $\frac{1}{6} + \frac{1}{6} \cdot \frac{1}{2}$.

If equal throws go for nothing, A's expectation after an equal throw clearly remains at e. In that case his expectation if he throws a 2 is $\frac{1}{6} + \frac{1}{6}e$.

We therefore have the following scheme:

A's throw	Chance thereof	A's expectation if equal throws divide the stake	A's expectation if equal throws go for nothing
2	$\frac{1}{6}$	$\frac{1}{6} + \frac{1}{6} \cdot \frac{1}{2}$	$\frac{1}{6} + \frac{1}{6}e$
3	$\frac{1}{6}$	$\frac{1}{3} + \frac{1}{6} \cdot \frac{1}{2}$	$\frac{1}{3} + \frac{1}{6}e$
4	$\frac{1}{6}$	$\frac{1}{2} + \frac{1}{6} \cdot \frac{1}{2}$	$\frac{1}{2} + \frac{1}{6}e$
5	$\frac{1}{6}$	$\frac{2}{3} + \frac{1}{6} \cdot \frac{1}{2}$	$\frac{2}{3} + \frac{1}{6}e$
6	$\frac{1}{6}$	$\frac{5}{6} + \frac{1}{6} \cdot \frac{1}{2}$	$\frac{5}{6} + \frac{1}{6}e$
7	$\frac{1}{6}$	1	1

The total expectation being the sum of the separate expectations, we have in the first case $e = \frac{47}{72}$, being the sum of the figures in the third column of the above table, and in the second case $e = \frac{7}{12} + \frac{5}{36}e$.

Whence $e = \frac{21}{31}$.

(v) A man tosses 20 pennies and removes all that fall head up; he then tosses the remainder and then removes all that fall head up, and so on. How many times ought he to be allowed to repeat this operation if he is to have an even chance of removing all the pennies before he has finished? [1906, Paper I, Q. 11.]

The problem is clearly the same if *all* the pennies are tossed each time; we then have to find the chance that all the pennies have turned up heads *once at least*.

If n be the required number of throws, the chance that any particular penny has turned up heads once at least is $\{1 - (\frac{1}{2})^n\}$.

The chance that *all* the pennies have turned up heads once at least is therefore $\{1 - (\frac{1}{2})^n\}^{20}$ and by the terms of the question this must equal $\frac{1}{2}$.

Solving this equation we find $(\frac{1}{2})^n = 1 - (\frac{1}{2})^{\frac{1}{20}}$,

$$n = 4\cdot87.$$

(vi) 2^n players of equal skill enter for a tournament; they are drawn in pairs, and the winners of each round are drawn again for the next. Find the probability that two given competitors will play against each other in the course of the tournament. If $n = 5$, show that the probability that a given player will either win or be beaten by the actual winner is $\frac{3}{16}$. [1912, Paper I, Q. 6.]

As regards the first part of the question, the total number of games that will be played is

$$2^{n-1} + 2^{n-2} + \ldots + 1 = 2^n - 1.$$

Also two players can be selected in $\dfrac{2^n(2^n - 1)}{2}$ ways. The chance that two will meet is therefore the quotient of these two values, i.e. $\dfrac{1}{2^{n-1}}$.

The second part of the question can be proved by an inductive process.

Let u_n be the required chance.

Then in the first round he may either win or lose. If he wins, he passes into the next round and his chance of winning or being beaten by the ultimate winner then becomes u_{n-1}. If he loses, his opponent passes into the next round where the latter's chance of becoming the ultimate winner is increased to $\dfrac{1}{2^{n-1}}$.

We thus have

$$u_n = \frac{1}{2} u_{n-1} + \frac{1}{2} \cdot \frac{1}{2^{n-1}}.$$

Similarly
$$\frac{1}{2} u_{n-1} = \frac{1}{4} u_{n-2} + \frac{1}{4} \cdot \frac{1}{2^{n-2}},$$

$$\frac{1}{4} u_{n-2} = \frac{1}{8} u_{n-3} + \frac{1}{8} \cdot \frac{1}{2^{n-3}},$$

etc.   etc.

$$\frac{1}{2^{n-2}} u_2 = \frac{1}{2^{n-1}} u_1 + \frac{1}{2^{n-1}} \cdot \frac{1}{2}.$$

As u_1 obviously equals 1, we have by addition

$$u_n = \frac{1}{2^{n-1}} + \frac{n-1}{2^n} = \frac{n+1}{2^n},$$

$$u_5 = \tfrac{3}{16}.$$

It is instructive also to prove the first part of the question inductively.

Let u_n be the required chance. This chance is compounded of the two chances that they meet in the first round, or that, not having met in the first round, they both pass into the second round where the corresponding chance becomes u_{n-1}.

The chance that they meet in the first round is $\dfrac{1}{2^n - 1}$; the chance that they do not meet is $\dfrac{2^n - 2}{2^n - 1}$. Therefore we have

$$u_n = \frac{1}{2^n - 1} + u_{n-1} \cdot \frac{1}{4} \cdot \frac{2^n - 2}{2^n - 1},$$

or
$$(2^n - 1) u_n = 1 + \frac{2^{n-1} - 1}{2} u_{n-1}.$$

Similarly
$$\left(\frac{2^{n-1} - 1}{2}\right) u_{n-1} = \frac{1}{2} + \frac{2^{n-2} - 1}{4} u_{n-2},$$

$$\left(\frac{2^{n-2} - 1}{4}\right) u_{n-2} = \frac{1}{4} + \frac{2^{n-3} - 1}{8} u_{n-3},$$

etc.   etc.

$$\left(\frac{2^3 - 1}{2^{n-3}}\right) u_3 = \frac{1}{2^{n-3}} + \frac{2^2 - 1}{2^{n-2}} u_2,$$

$$\left(\frac{2^2 - 1}{2^{n-2}}\right) u_2 = \frac{1}{2^{n-2}} + \frac{2 - 1}{2^{n-1}} u_1.$$

By addition

$$(2^n - 1) u_n = 1 + \frac{1}{2} + \frac{1}{4} + \ldots + \frac{1}{2^{n-2}} + \frac{1}{2^{n-1}}$$

(since u_1 obviously equals 1)

$$= \frac{1 - \dfrac{1}{2^n}}{1 - \dfrac{1}{2}} = \frac{2^n - 1}{2^{n-1}}.$$

Whence
$$u_n = \frac{1}{2^{n-1}},$$

as before.

16. The application of the Integral Calculus to problems of mean value and probability is shown in Chapter XIX, §§ 5–7.

EXAMPLES

CHAPTER III

1. Given
$$f(1)=(x-2)(x-3), \quad f(2)=(x-7)(x-5), \quad f(3)=(x-10)(x+1), \quad f(4)=63,$$
obtain a value for x, assuming second differences are constant.

2. Find the nth term of the series 2, 12, 36, 98, 270, 768, etc. and the sum of n terms of it.

3. Given that
$$f(0)=66566, \quad f(1)=65152, \quad f(2)=63677, \quad f(3)=62136,$$
find $f(9)$.

4. Find
$$\Delta^{20} \frac{6x+29}{(3x+1)(3x+4)(3x+7)(3x+10)}.$$

5. Find the value of
$$\Delta^n (3x+1)(3x+4)(3x+7) \ldots (3x+3n-2).$$

6. Prove that
$$(n-1)^m f(x) + m(n-1)^{m-1} f(x+1) + \frac{m(m-1)}{2!}(n-1)^{m-2} f(x+2)$$
$$+ \ldots + f(x+m) = n^m f(x) + mn^{m-1} \Delta f(x)$$
$$+ \frac{m(m-1)}{2!} n^{m-2} \Delta^2 f(x) + \ldots + \Delta^m f(x).$$

Hence find the sum of the series
$$1^2 + m \cdot 2^2 + \frac{m(m-1)}{2!} 3^2 + \ldots + (m+1)^2.$$

CHAPTER IV

1. Given
$$f(0)=70795, \quad f(1)=72444, \quad f(2)=74131, \text{ and } f(6)=81283,$$
find $f(3), f(4)$, and $f(5)$.

2. Find $f(35)$ given
$$f(20)=\cdot01313, \quad f(30)=\cdot01727, \quad f(40)=\cdot02392, \quad f(50)=\cdot03493.$$

3. Supply the missing term in the following table:
$$f(0)=72795,$$
$$f(1)=71651,$$
$$f(2)=70458,$$

$$f(4)=67919,$$
$$f(5)=66566,$$
$$f(6)=65152.$$

4. Given
$$f(0)=11, \quad f(3)=18, \quad f(6)=74, \text{ and } f(9)=522,$$
find the intermediate terms.

5. Given

$$f(0) = 98203, \quad f(1) = 97843, \quad f(2) = 97459, \quad f(3) = 97034,$$

find $f(2\cdot25)$.

6. Given

$$f(0) = 98023, \quad f(10) = 97651, \quad f(20) = 97246, \quad f(30) = 96802,$$

find $f(15)$.

7. Given

$$f(0) = 58\cdot842, \quad f(2) = 55\cdot257, \quad f(4) = 51\cdot368, \quad f(10) = 37\cdot977,$$

complete the series $f(0), f(1), \dots f(10)$.

8. If you were asked at very short notice to obtain approximate values for the complete series $f(0), f(1), f(2), \dots f(20)$, being given that $f(0) = \cdot013$, $f(10) = \cdot248$, $f(15) = \cdot578$, and $f(20) = \cdot983$, what methods would you adopt, and what value would you obtain for $f(9)$?

9. $f(1) = 1; \quad f(2) + f(3) = 5\cdot41; \quad f(4) + f(5) + f(6) = 18\cdot47;$

         $f(7) + f(8) + f(9) + f(10) + f(11) + f(12) = 90\cdot36.$

Find the value of $f(x)$ for all values of x from 1 to 12 inclusive.

10. Apply Lagrange's formula to find $f(5)$ and $f(6)$, given that

$$f(1) = 2, \quad f(2) = 4, \quad f(3) = 8, \quad f(4) = 16 \text{ and } f(7) = 128;$$

and explain why the results differ from those obtained by completing the series of powers of 2.

11. Find the simplest algebraic expression in x which has the values 5, 3, 9, 47 and 165 when x has the values 0, 1, 2, 3 and 4 respectively.

12. Prove the following formulas for approximate interpolation:

$$f(1) = f(3) - \cdot3\,[f(5) - f(-3)] + \cdot2\,[f(-3) - f(-5)] \quad \dots\dots\dots(1),$$

$$f(0) = \tfrac{1}{2}[f(1) + f(-1)] - \tfrac{1}{8}[\tfrac{1}{2}\{f(3) - f(1)\} - \tfrac{1}{2}\{f(-1) - f(-3)\}] \dots(2),$$

and apply them to find the logs of 45, 46, 47, 48, 49, being given

$$\log 42 = 1\cdot62325, \quad \log 50 = 1\cdot69897,$$

$$\log 44 = 1\cdot64345, \quad \log 52 = 1\cdot71600.$$

13. Given

$$\overset{10}{\underset{1}{\Sigma}} f(x) = 500426, \quad \overset{10}{\underset{4}{\Sigma}} f(x) = 329240, \quad \overset{10}{\underset{7}{\Sigma}} f(x) = 175212 \text{ and } f(10) = 40365,$$

find $f(1)$.

CHAPTER V

1. Use Gauss' interpolation formula to obtain the value of $f(41)$ given

$$f(30) = 3678\cdot2, \quad f(35) = 2995\cdot1, \quad f(40) = 2400\cdot1,$$

$$f(45) = 1876\cdot2, \quad f(50) = 1416\cdot3.$$

Verify your result by using Lagrange's formula over the same figures.

2. Given the following table find $f(28)$ using Stirling's formula:

$$f(20)=98450, \quad f(25)=96632, \quad f(30)=94472,$$
$$f(35)=91852, \quad f(40)=88613.$$

3. Prove that

$$f(x)=\tfrac{1}{2}[f(-\tfrac{1}{2})+f(\tfrac{1}{2})]+x\Delta f(-\tfrac{1}{2})+\frac{x^2-\tfrac{1}{4}}{2!}\cdot\frac{\Delta^2 f(-\tfrac{3}{2})+\Delta^2 f(-\tfrac{1}{2})}{2}+\ldots,$$

and apply the formula to find $f(32)$ given

$$f(25)=\cdot2707, \quad f(30)=\cdot3027, \quad f(35)=\cdot3386, \quad f(40)=\cdot3794.$$

4. From the table of annual net premiums given below find the annual net premium at age 25 by means of Bessel's formula:

Age	Annual Net Premiums
20	·01427
24	·01581
28	·01772
32	·01996

5. Use Everett's interpolation formula to complete the series $f(25)$ to $f(35)$, given that

$$f(15)=305, \quad f(20)=457, \quad f(25)=568, \quad f(30)=671,$$
$$f(35)=897, \quad f(40)=1190, \quad f(45)=1481.$$

CHAPTER VI

1. Given the following table of $f(x)$:

$$f(0)=217, \quad f(1)=140, \quad f(2)=23, \quad f(3)=-6,$$

show how to find approximately the value of x for which the function is zero.

2. Given that, when

$$x=0, \quad f(x)=0,$$
$$x=1, \quad f(x)=100,$$
$$x=2, \quad f(x)=2000,$$

find x when $f(x)=1900$ by Lagrange's formula of interpolation (applied inversely) and explain why the result does not agree with that found by using the formula $f(x)=(1+\Delta)^x f(0)$ and solving the quadratic.

3. The following values of $f(x)$ are given:

$$f(10)=1754, \quad f(15)=2648, \quad f(20)=3564.$$

Find, correct to one decimal place, the value of x for which $f(x)=3000$.

4. $\qquad f(30)=-30, \quad f(34)=-13, \quad f(38)=3, \quad f(42)=18.$

Apply Lagrange's formula of interpolation inversely to find x, where $f(x)=0$.

CHAPTER VII

1. Find the value of

$$\Delta^{-1} \frac{1}{n\,(n+1)\,(n+2) \ldots (n+r-1)},$$

and use the result to find the value of

$$\sum_{2}^{7} \frac{1}{n\,(n+1)\,(n+2)}.$$

2. Prove that

$$\sum_{1}^{n} (x^2+1)\,.\,x! = n\,.\,(n+1)!.$$

3. Show that

$$\Sigma a^x \phi(x) = \frac{a^x}{a-1}\left[\phi(x) - \frac{a}{a-1}\,\Delta\phi(x) + \frac{a^2}{(a-1)^2}\,\Delta^2\phi(x) - \ldots\right],$$

where $\phi(x)$ is any rational integral algebraic function of x.

4. Prove that if a_n diminishes as n increases and converges to the limit zero, the sum to infinity of the series $a_1 - a_2 + a_3 \ldots$ is the same as the sum to infinity of the series $\frac{1}{2}a_1 - \frac{1}{4}\Delta a_2 + \frac{1}{8}\Delta^2 a_3 - $ etc.

Find the sum to infinity of the series $\frac{1}{10} - \frac{1}{11} + \frac{1}{12} \ldots$ true to four decimal places.

5. Prove that if the fourth and higher differences are ignored the sum of n successive terms of a function of which $f(0)$ is the central term is

$$nf(0) + \frac{n^3-n}{24}\,\Delta^2 f(-1),$$

where n is an odd number.

CHAPTER VIII

1. Given the following values of $f(x)$:
$$f(1\cdot41) = \cdot7092, \quad f(1\cdot49) = \cdot6711,$$
$$f(1\cdot52) = \cdot6579, \quad f(1\cdot53) = \cdot6536,$$
find $f(1\cdot45)$.

2. Use Divided Differences to find $f(80)$ to the nearest integer, given
$$f(70) = 235, \quad f(71) = 256, \quad f(79) = 436, \quad f(81) = 484.$$

3. Given
$$f(20) = \cdot342, \quad f(23) = \cdot391, \quad f(31) = \cdot515, \quad f(34) = \cdot559,$$
find $f(30)$ by means of Divided Differences, and check the result by applying Lagrange's interpolation formula.

CHAPTER IX

1. The following values of $f(x, y)$ are given:

$$f(35, 55) = 10\cdot020, \quad f(35, 50) = 11\cdot196, \quad f(35, 45) = 12\cdot019,$$
$$f(40, 55) = 9\cdot796, \quad f(40, 50) = 10\cdot894, \quad f(40, 45) = 11\cdot641,$$
$$f(45, 55) = 9\cdot583, \quad f(45, 50) = 10\cdot591, \quad f(45, 45) = 11\cdot243.$$

(i) Using only six of the above values, find $f(42, 52)$.

(ii) Making use of all the data calculate $f(44, 51)$.

2. Prove that if $f(0, 1) = f(1, 0)$ and $f(0, 2) = f(2, 0)$, then

$$f(x, y) = f(0, 0) + (x+y)\left[\Delta_x + \frac{x+y-1}{2}\Delta^2_x\right]f(0, 0) + xy\left[f(1, 1) - f(2, 0)\right].$$

Find $f(39, 33)$, given

$$f(35, 35) = 3\cdot151, \quad f(35, 45) = 3\cdot912,$$
$$f(35, 40) = 3\cdot471, \quad f(40, 40) = 3\cdot766.$$

CHAPTER XI

1. Find the differential coefficients with regard to x of $\log x^{\frac{1}{x}}$ and

$$\frac{\sqrt{x^2-3}}{(x-1)\sqrt{x^2-7}}.$$

2. Differentiate with respect to x

$$\log \sqrt[3]{\frac{a^3 + a^2x + ax^2 + x^3}{a^2 + ax + x^2}}.$$

3. Find the differential coefficient with regard to x^2 of

$$\frac{\sqrt{x^2-2}}{x}.$$

4. Differentiate

(1) $a^x \left(\dfrac{x}{a}\right)^{ax} \log \dfrac{x}{a}$, with respect to $\log \dfrac{x}{a}$,

(2) $\log \dfrac{xe^x}{e^x-1}$, with respect to x,

(3) $x^{(\log x)^2}$, with respect to x.

5. If $(1-x)^y + (1-y)^x = 0$, find $\dfrac{dy}{dx}$.

6. Obtain the differential coefficients of

(1) $\log \dfrac{x}{a^x}$, (2) e^{x^x}, with respect to x.

CHAPTER XII

1. Find (1) the nth differential coefficient of $\dfrac{1}{(x+1)(x^2-1)}$ with respect to x, and (2) the second differential coefficient of $\log_a(1+x)$ with respect to $\log_e x$.

2. Find the nth differential coefficient of $e^{ax}(x-2)^2$.

3. Having given that

$$x^2\frac{d^2y}{dx^2}+x\frac{dy}{dx}+y=0,$$

prove that $\quad x^2\dfrac{d^{n+2}y}{dx^{n+2}}+(2n+1)x\cdot\dfrac{d^{n+1}y}{dx^{n+1}}+(n^2+1)\dfrac{d^ny}{dx^n}=0.$

4. Obtain the second differential coefficient of $\log(a+bx+cx^2)$ with respect to $\sqrt{x}$.

5. Find the nth differential coefficient with respect to x of

$$\frac{x+1}{2x^2-5x+3}.$$

CHAPTER XIII

1. Prove that $\qquad \dfrac{x}{e^x-1}=1-\dfrac{x}{2}+\dfrac{x^2}{12}-\dfrac{x^4}{720}\cdots$

and show that no odd power of x beyond the first can occur.

2. Prove that $\quad \dfrac{\log(x+\sqrt{1+x^2})}{\sqrt{1+x^2}}=x-\tfrac{2}{3}x^3+\dfrac{2.4}{3.5}x^5-\dots.$

3. Prove that the first three terms of the expansion of $(1+x)^{\frac{1}{x}}$ in powers of x are $e-\dfrac{ex}{2}+\tfrac{11}{24}ex^2$.

4. Expand $\log(x+\sqrt{a^2+x^2})$ in ascending powers of x.

5. Expand $\dfrac{\log(1+x^2)}{e^x-1}$ in ascending powers of x as far as the term involving x^6.

CHAPTER XIV

1. Evaluate $\qquad \underset{x\to 0}{\text{Lt}}\left[\dfrac{\log(1+x)}{e^x-1}\right].$

2. Find the maximum value of $x(x-1)(x-2)$ between the limits 0 and 1.

3. Find the values of x at the points where the graph of the function $(1+x^2)e^{1-x^2}$ has its greatest slope.

4. A man in a boat at sea, 5 miles distant from the nearest point of a straight shore, wishes to reach a place 12 miles distant along the shore, measuring from this nearest point. At what point should he land to reach this place in the minimum time, if he can row at 3 miles an hour and walk at 4 miles an hour?

5. Given $f(0)=1876$, $f(1)=777$, $f(3)=19$, and $f(6)=-218$, interpolate the values of $f(2)$, $f(4)$, and $f(5)$ and find the values of x for which $f(x)$ is a maximum or minimum.

6. Find the minimum and maximum values of

$$x^4 - 4x^3 - 8x^2 + 48x - 48.$$

7. A window is in shape a rectangle with a semicircle covering the top. If the perimeter of the window be a fixed length l, find what is its maximum area.

8. Find
                    (1) $\underset{x \to a}{\text{Lt}}\ \dfrac{x - a + \sqrt{x^m - a^m}}{\sqrt{x^n - a^n}}$,

                    (2) $\underset{x \to 0}{\text{Lt}}\ (1 + x^3)^{\frac{1}{x^2}}$.

CHAPTER XV

1. Show that $\dfrac{d^3 f(x)}{dx^3} = \Delta^3 f(x - \tfrac{3}{2})$ approximately.

By considering the function $f(x) = a + bx + c^x$ and using the above relation prove that $\log_e c = c^{\frac{1}{2}} - c^{-\frac{1}{2}}$ approximately, where c is a small quantity.

2. Show that $\Delta 0^m - \dfrac{\Delta^2}{2} 0^m + \dfrac{\Delta^3}{3} 0^m \ldots = 0$, when $m > 1$.

3. Prove that, if $f(x)$ be a function the fourth differences of which are constant,

$$\frac{df(x)}{dx} = \tfrac{1}{12}[f(x-2) - 8f(x-1) + 8f(x+1) - f(x+2)]$$

and hence find an approximate value for $\dfrac{d}{dx}[\log f(x)]$ where

$$f(x-2) = 42{\cdot}699, \quad f(x-1) = 40{\cdot}365, \quad f(x) = 37{\cdot}977,$$
$$f(x+1) = 35{\cdot}543, \quad f(x+2) = 33{\cdot}075.$$

CHAPTER XVIII

1. Find the integrals

    (1) $\displaystyle\int \frac{x^3}{\sqrt{x-1}}\, dx.$ (2) $\displaystyle\int \frac{x^2}{x^6 - a^6}\, dx.$ (3) $\displaystyle\int \frac{\log(\log x)}{x}\, dx.$

2. Evaluate $\displaystyle\int x^4 a^x\, dx.$

3. Evaluate

$$(1) \int \sqrt{x^2 + 2ax}\, dx. \qquad (2) \int \frac{x^3\, dx}{(a^2 - x^2)^{\frac{1}{2}}}. \qquad (3) \int \frac{\log x\, dx}{(1 - x)^2}.$$

4. Find the value of $\displaystyle \int \frac{27x^2 - 171x + 256}{2\,(x - 3)^3\,(x + 4)}\, dx.$

5. Evaluate

$$\int \frac{4x + 2}{(x - 1)^2\,(x - 7)}\, dx \ ; \qquad \int \log(1 - x^2)\, dx \ ; \qquad \int x^n\,(\log x)^3\, dx.$$

CHAPTER XIX

1. If $f(x) = a + bx + cx^2$, find expressions for $f(\frac{1}{2})$, $\dfrac{df(0)}{dx}$ and $\displaystyle \int_0^1 f(x)\, dx$ in terms of $f(0)$, $f(1)$ and $f(2)$.

2. Evaluate $\displaystyle \int_0^1 \frac{x^3}{(2x + 1)^5}\, dx.$

3. Find the value of $\displaystyle \int_{\frac{1}{2}}^1 \frac{2x^2 + 9x - 2}{x\,(2 - x)\,(x + 1)}\, dx.$

4. Find the average value of $x\,(x - 1)\,(x - 2)$ between the limits 0 and 1.

5. Find the value of $\displaystyle \int_0^1 x^{2n-1} e^{x^n}\, dx.$

CHAPTER XX

1. From the table

$$f(0) = 217, \quad f(1) = 140, \quad f(2) = 23, \quad f(3) = -6,$$

find an approximate value for $\displaystyle \int_0^3 f(x)\, dx$, and explain why the result differs from $f(0) + f(1) + f(2) + f(3)$.

2. Prove that approximately

$$\int_{-\frac{1}{2}}^{+\frac{1}{2}} f(x)\, dx = \tfrac{1}{24}\,\{f(-1) + 22f(0) + f(1)\},$$

and find thereby an approximate value for

$$\int_{\frac{1}{2}}^{1\frac{1}{2}} 10{,}000 \times 4^{-x} \times 2^{3^x}\, dx.$$

3. Discuss the error in assuming that

$$\int_0^1 f(x)\, dx = f(\tfrac{1}{2}) = \tfrac{1}{2}\,[f(0) + f(1)]$$

if (1) $f(x) = a + bx + cx^2$, (2) $f(x) = 100 \times 4^x$.

4. Given $f(-2)$, $f(0)$, $f(2)$, find an approximate value for

$$\int_{-3}^3 f(x)\, dx.$$

5. Prove that

$$\int_0^1 f(x)\,dx = \tfrac{1}{12}\left[5f(1) + 8f(0) - f(-1)\right] \text{ approximately.}$$

If the speed of a train on a non-stop run is as shown in the table below, find the approximate mileage travelled between 12.0 and 12.30, using the above formula.

Time	Speed in miles per hour
11.50	24·2
12.0	35·0
12.10	41·3
12.20	42·8
12.30	39·2

6. If $f(1) = 4157$, $f(2) = 4527$, $f(4) = 5435$, find approximately the value of

$$\int_1^4 f(x)\,dx.$$

CHAPTER XXI

1. n persons are sitting at a round table, and from them three are selected at random; show that the chance that no two of those selected are sitting next one another is $\dfrac{(n-4)(n-5)}{(n-1)(n-2)}$.

2. A heap of playing cards contains 6 hearts, 5 spades and 4 clubs. A card is chosen at random 9 times in succession and is not replaced. Find the chance (1) that there are no hearts left, and (2) only hearts are left.

3. A man has two sovereigns and four shillings in his pocket; from these he selects at random 3 coins, and again chooses from these 3 coins at random, the first coin for A, the second for B, and the third for C.

Find the values of the expectations of A, B, and C.

4. Find the probability that out of 5 persons aged 45 exactly 3 will die in a year.

Probability that a person aged 45 will die in a year = ·01224.

5. A die with six faces is thrown three times and the sum of the throws is twelve: find the chance (1) that the first throw was a four: (2) that four was thrown each time.

6. Two men, A and B, each draw a card from a well-shuffled pack of playing cards, find that they are of the same value, and replace the cards; they do this four times in succession. Find the chance that this would happen and show that it is approximately $\dfrac{1}{84,000}$.

7. The probability that a man aged 50 will survive one year is ·98428. Show that the probability that, out of 5 men aged 50, 3 at least will die within a year is ·0000385.

8. The 26 letters of the alphabet are placed in a bag. A and B alternately draw a letter from the bag, the letters drawn not being replaced. The winner is the one who draws most vowels. A starts and draws a vowel with his first draw. What is his chance of winning?

9. If a number of five figures containing any five of the ten digits once only is written down at random, what is the probability that it is divisible by 9?

10. Given the following table find the probability that one at least of three persons aged respectively 20, 30, 40 will die between the 10th and 20th year from now :

Age	Probability of surviving 10 years	Probability of surviving 20 years
20	·93363	·85651
30	·91740	·81167
40	·88476	·71517

11. Two persons, A and B, play for a stake, each throwing alternately two dice, A commencing. A wins if he throws six, B if he throws seven, the game ceasing as soon as either event happens. What ratio will A's chance of winning bear to B's?

12. The sum of two positive integers (excluding zero) is 100; find the chance that their product exceeds 1200.

13. The following table shows the probability that a woman of the age specified will marry in a year:

Age	Probability of marriage
20	·0665
25	·1033
30	·0649
40	·0183

Find the probability that, out of 4 women aged 20, 25, 30, 40 respectively, only one marries within a year.

14. A bag contains 8 counters, numbered 1 to 8. Four are drawn at random. Find the chances that

(1) The sum of the numbers on the four counters amounts to at least 17.

(2) The counters numbered 2 and 3 are among the four.

(3) The four counters contain at least two of the three counters numbered 3, 5 and 7.

15. A penny is tossed six times. Find the chance that neither heads nor tails have occurred three times in succession.

16. An urn contains counters marked with the digits 6, 7, 8 and 9; and the number of times each digit occurs is equal to the value of the digit. If counters are drawn one at a time, each counter being replaced when drawn, what is the probability

(1) that the digit 6 is drawn before the digit 9;

(2) that the sum of the first three digits drawn is exactly 20?

17. A and B play a set of games, to be won by the player who first wins four games, with the condition that if they each win three they are to play the best of three to decide the set. A's chance of winning a single game is to B's as 2 to 1. Find their respective chances of winning the set.

18. The probability of any one of 10 men each aged 30 surviving a year is ·99229.

Show that the probability that exactly 5 men out of the 10 survive a year is $6·6 \times 10^{-9}$.

Find also the probability that of the 10 men one particular man will die first and another particular man last.

19. A point is taken at random within the area bounded by the curve $y = x \log x$, the x axis, and the ordinates at the points $x = 1$, and $x = 4$.

Find the probability that the distance of the point from the y axis is less than 2.

20. In a game of whist the dealer found that on turning up the last card he had the Ace, King, Queen, Knave, Ten, and 3 other trumps in his hand. Find the chance that this would occur.

21. A and B cut a pack of cards, the player who wins the cut six times to be the winner. A, having won four times to B's once, cuts a five. Find the chance that A will be the winner.

22. In a line AB of length $3a$, a point P is taken at random and then in AP a point Q is taken at random. What is the probability that PQ exceeds a?

ANSWERS TO EXAMPLES

CHAPTER III

1. $x = 12$ or -16.
2. nth term $= n^2 + n - 3 + 3^n$. Sum of n terms $= \dfrac{2n^3 + 6n^2 - 14n - 9}{6} + \dfrac{3^{n+1}}{2}$.
3. 51224.
4. $\dfrac{3^{20}}{2} \cdot 22\,! \cdot \dfrac{6x + 209}{(3x+1)(3x+4)\ldots(3x+70)}$.
5. $3^n \cdot n\,!$.
6. $2^{m-2}(m+1)(m+4)$.

CHAPTER IV

1. $f(3) = 75857\cdot2$; $f(4) = 77623\cdot8$; $f(5) = 79432\cdot0$.
2. $\cdot02017$.
3. 69215.
4. 12, 14; 26, 42; 138, 266.
5. 97357.
6. 97453.
7. $\Delta f(0) = -1\cdot753875$, $\Delta^2 f(0) = -\cdot07725$ and $\Delta^3 f(0) = \cdot00125$ from which the series may be completed.
8. $\cdot1954$.
9. $\Delta f(1) = 1\cdot1006$, $\Delta^2 f(1) = \cdot1083$ and $\Delta^3 f(1) = \cdot0137$ from which the values of $f(x)$ required may be found.
10. $f(5) = 32\tfrac{14}{15}$; $f(6) = 66\tfrac{2}{3}$.
11. $x^4 - 2x^3 + 3x^2 - 4x + 5$ or $24 \cdot 2^x - 8x^2 - 18x - 19$.
12. $\log 45 = 1\cdot65321$, $\quad \log 46 = 1\cdot66276$, $\quad \log 47 = 1\cdot67210$, $\log 48 = 1\cdot68125$, $\quad \log 49 = 1\cdot69020$.
13. $58843\tfrac{46}{81}$.

CHAPTER V

1. $2290\cdot0$.
2. 95384.
3. $\cdot3165$.
4. $\cdot01625$.
5. The series is $f(25)\ 568,\quad f(26)\ 585,\quad f(27)\ 602,\quad f(28)\ 621,$
$f(29)\ 644,\quad f(30)\ 671,\quad f(31)\ 707,\quad f(32)\ 747,$
$f(33)\ 793,\quad f(34)\ 843,\quad f(35)\ 897.$

CHAPTER VI

1. $2\cdot751$.
2. $2\tfrac{4}{5}$.
3. $16\cdot9$.
4. $37\cdot2$.

CHAPTER VII

1. $\dfrac{1}{1-r} \cdot \dfrac{1}{n(n+1)(n+2)\ldots(n+r-2)}$; $\dfrac{11}{144}$.
4. $\cdot0525$.

CHAPTER VIII

1. $\cdot6895$.
2. 460.
3. $\cdot500$.

CHAPTER IX

1. (i) $10\cdot389$; (ii) $10\cdot475$.   2. $3\cdot297$.

CHAPTER XI

1. $\dfrac{1}{x^2}(1-\log x)$; $\dfrac{-x^4+6x^2+4x-21}{(x-1)^2(x^2-3)^{\frac{1}{2}}(x^2-7)^{\frac{2}{3}}}$.

2. $\dfrac{x^2(3a^2+2ax+x^2)}{3(a+x)(a^2+x^2)(a^2+ax+x^2)}$.   3. $\dfrac{1}{x^3\sqrt{x^2-2}}$.

4. (1) $a^x\left(\dfrac{x}{a}\right)^{ax}\left[x\log a \cdot \log\dfrac{x}{a}+ax\log\dfrac{x}{a}\left(\log\dfrac{x}{a}+1\right)+1\right]$,

    (2) $\dfrac{1}{x}-\dfrac{1}{e^x-1}$,   (3) $\dfrac{3x^{(\log x)^2}(\log x)^2}{x}$.

5. $-\dfrac{y(1-x)^{y-1}-(1-y)^x\log(1-y)}{x(1-y)^{x-1}-(1-x)^y\log(1-x)}$.   6. $\dfrac{1}{x}-\log a$; $e^{xx}x^x(\log x+1)$.

CHAPTER XII

1. (1) $\dfrac{(-1)^n\cdot n!}{4}\left[\dfrac{1}{(x-1)^{n+1}}-\dfrac{1}{(x+1)^{n+1}}-\dfrac{2(n+1)}{(x+1)^{n+2}}\right]$; (2) $\dfrac{x\log_a e}{(1+x)^2}$.

2. $e^{ax}\cdot a^{n-2}[a^2(x-2)^2+2na(x-2)+n(n-1)]$.

4. $2\dfrac{[ab+x(6ca-b^2)-bcx^2-2c^2x^3]}{(a+bx+cx^2)^2}$.

5. $(-1)^n\cdot n!\left[\dfrac{5\cdot2^n}{(2x-3)^{n+1}}-\dfrac{2}{(x-1)^{n+1}}\right]$.

CHAPTER XIII

4. $\log a+\dfrac{x}{a}-\dfrac{x^3}{6a^3}+\dfrac{3x^5}{40a^5}-\ldots+(-1)^r\dfrac{1\cdot3\ldots(2r-1)\,x^{2r+1}}{r!\,(2r+1)\,2^r\,a^{2r+1}}+\ldots$.

5. $x-\dfrac{x^2}{2}-\dfrac{5x^3}{12}+\dfrac{x^4}{4}+\dfrac{209x^5}{720}$.

CHAPTER XIV

1. 1.   2. $\dfrac{2}{3\sqrt{3}}$.   3. $\pm\sqrt{\dfrac{3}{2}}$.   4. $\dfrac{15}{\sqrt{7}}$ miles from the nearest point

5. $f(2)=218$, $f(4)=0$, $f(5)=-19$.

    Maximum value when $x=\dfrac{120+\sqrt{110}}{30}$.

    Minimum value when $x=\dfrac{120-\sqrt{110}}{30}$.

6. Minimum values -3, -128. Maximum value 0.

7. $\dfrac{l^2}{2(\pi+4)}$.   8. (1) $\sqrt{\dfrac{m}{n}}\cdot a^{m-n}$; (2) 1.

CHAPTER XV

3. $-\cdot06353$.

CHAPTER XVIII

1. (1) $\dfrac{2\sqrt{x-1}}{35}(5x^3+6x^2+8x+16)+c$; (2) $\dfrac{1}{6a^3}\log\left(\dfrac{x^3-a^3}{x^3+a^3}\right)+c$;

(3) $\log x\,[\log(\log x)-1]+c$.

2. $a^x\left[\dfrac{x^4}{\log_e a}-\dfrac{4x^3}{(\log_e a)^2}+\dfrac{12x^2}{(\log_e a)^3}-\dfrac{24x}{(\log_e a)^4}+\dfrac{24}{(\log_e a)^5}\right]+c$.

3. (1) $\tfrac{1}{2}\left[(x+a)\sqrt{x^2+2ax}-a^2\log\{(x+a)+\sqrt{x^2+2ax}\}+c\right]$;

(2) $\tfrac{1}{3}(a^2-x^2)^{\frac{3}{2}}-a^2\sqrt{a^2-x^2}+c$; (3) $\dfrac{x\log x}{1-x}+\log(1-x)+c$.

4. $\dfrac{x-2}{2(x-3)^2}+2\log\dfrac{x-3}{x+4}+c$.

5. $\log\left(\dfrac{x-7}{x-1}\right)^{\frac{5}{6}}+\dfrac{1}{x-1}+c$; $(1+x)\log(1+x)-(1-x)\log(1-x)-2x+c$;

$\dfrac{x^{n+1}}{(n+1)^4}[\{(n+1)\log x\}^3-3\{(n+1)\log x\}^2+6(n+1)\log x-6]+c$.

CHAPTER XIX

1. $\tfrac{1}{3}[3f(0)+6f(1)-f(2)]$; $\tfrac{1}{2}[-3f(0)+4f(1)-f(2)]$;
$\tfrac{1}{12}[5f(0)+8f(1)-f(2)]$.

2. $\tfrac{1}{324}$.　　　3. $\log_e 6$.　　　4. $\tfrac{1}{4}$.　　　5. $\dfrac{1}{n}$.

CHAPTER XX

1. $262\tfrac{1}{2}$.　　　2. 32500.　　　3. (1) $-\tfrac{1}{12}c$; $\tfrac{1}{6}c$.　(2) $-16\cdot5$; $33\cdot5$.
4. $\tfrac{3}{4}[3f(-2)+2f(0)+3f(2)]$.　　　5. $20\cdot4$ miles.　　　6. 14262.

CHAPTER XXI

2. (1) $\tfrac{12}{715}$; (2) $\tfrac{1}{5005}$.　　　3. $7s.\,4d.,\,7s.\,4d.,\,7s.\,4d.$　　　4. $\cdot0000179$.
5. (1) $\tfrac{1}{6}$; (2) $\tfrac{1}{25}$.　　　6. $\tfrac{1}{83521}$.　　　8. $\tfrac{773}{1150}$.
9. $\tfrac{1}{9}$.　　　10. $\cdot31466$.　　　11. $30:31$.　　　12. $\tfrac{73}{99}$.
13. $\cdot2109$.　　　14. (1) $\tfrac{23}{25}$; (2) $\tfrac{3}{14}$; (3) $\tfrac{1}{2}$.　　　15. $\tfrac{13}{32}$.
16. (1) $\tfrac{2}{5}$; (2) $\tfrac{27}{1000}$.　　　17. A's chance $\tfrac{16592}{19683}$; B's chance $\tfrac{3091}{19683}$.
18. $\cdot01111$.　　　19. $\dfrac{8\log 2-3}{64\log 2-15}$.　　　20. $\dfrac{101,232}{809,966,275}$.
21. $\tfrac{711}{832}$.　　　22. $\tfrac{2}{3}-\tfrac{1}{3}\log 3$.

CAMBRIDGE: PRINTED BY J. B. PEACE, M.A., AT THE UNIVERSITY PRESS.